NUISANCE ANIMALS

Backyard Pests to Free-Roaming Killers

John Trout, Jr.

Midwest Publishing

Library of Congress Catalog Card Number: 97-93613
ISBN 0-9636526-1-3

Trout, John Jr., 1946-
Nuisance Animals

Index: p.
Bibliography: p.
Appendix: p.

This book is affectionately dedicated to my four children,
Alisa, Tammy, Kathy and John.
Most of all, they support and understand
my devotion to wildlife.

Acknowledgments

Contributions from many organizations and individuals have made this book possible. Comments, literature and statistics they supplied are products of a great deal of their effort and time.

Let me start by saying thanks to the many wildlife, resource, animal damage control, transportation and agriculture agencies on the national, state and provincial levels. There are far too many to mention, but the valuable facts they provided became a must for this book.

My sincere thanks to my good friend and well-qualified editor, Dr. Jim Casada, who took my mumbo-jumbo mess and turned it into a presentable book.

Also, thanks to the U.S. Department of Agriculture Animal and Plant Health Inspection Service Animal Damage Control, the U.S. Fish and Wildlife Service and the Bureau of the Census for national statistics they contributed.

Ernie Provost, a wildlife professor at the University of Georgia, also contributed comments for the book. My appreciation should be extended to him even further, however, for the excellent job he has done of preserving wildlife habitat and educating individuals through his teachings and seminars.

In the Bibliography, you will see the titles of several publications. I thank the publisher and author of each for their valuable reference materials. The contents of these publications added information that you are sure to appreciate.

Finally, I wish to thank my wife Vikki for her contribution. While holding down a full-time job, she still made time for proofing the thousands of words beyond this page.

Contents

Introduction

As I write this introduction, a gray squirrel scampers up a stately white oak tree only yards from the window over my desk. Farther to the East, I can see a hardwood thicket that harbors a variety of wildlife species. I cannot see the animals that reside in the dense woods, but make no mistake, they are there. They live near me, and I live near them; we share the same environment.

It has been my good fortune to live in the suburbs or rural areas for almost three decades. During this period, I have come to know numerous animals — some were welcome, others that were not. That's what this book is about: coping with wildlife and its behavior, and understanding its needs as well as our own.

I have also enjoyed many years of camping, fishing, hiking, hunting and photographing wildlife in our wonderful outdoors. These activities have kept me closely attuned to nature as I study wildlife and learn its habits. My trade is almost as satisfying. I am a full-time outdoor writer and photographer. So, when I cannot pursue the outdoors on location, I can at least be writing about nature.

The title of this book in no way is meant to imply that animals are nuisances. On the contrary, animals provide us with contentment and well being. I enjoy watching them and admiring their habits whenever possible. However, in recent years mushrooming human populations have expanded deep into the animal's kingdom. We have also come to realize that animals will occasionally take it upon themselves to share our belongings or impose a danger. Thus, we must prevent the problem from recurring, either by controlling the nuisance animal or by making adjustments at the problem site.

Although this book's title uses the term animals, keep in mind that it will not discuss all wildlife found near our homes. Actually, there are several classes of wildlife. There are birds, fish, insects, mammals, reptiles and many more. In each classification there are hundreds or even thousands of species. Many backyard wildlife books discuss everything from butterflies to songbirds. I could not include every species that shares our surroundings, but I tried to make logical selections. This book will focus on common mammals that often become a nuisance, along with a few others that most of us would not expect to encounter near our homes. These are animals that share this busy world with us. Some of those we see, and some we do not.

In this book I elaborate on several topics. The book is not about saving wildlife, although it supports that theory while targeting those animals that become a hindrance. I admire animals and consider myself a conservationist. There is a lot said in this book about restoring wildlife habitat and what you can do to ensure the survival of many wildlife species. But I fully realize that we must deal with those animals that become a persistent nuisance. Most individuals have no idea where to begin when a problem occurs, whether it be an animal that obliterates the vegetable garden or one that kills the livestock. As the cover suggests, this book will help everyone living in suburbs, rural areas, and urban districts to understand many species of wildlife better and to deal with animal behavior. This book is chock-full of such information.

Early in this book you will read about many of the problems that have evolved from man and wildlife living together. Remember though, many species of wildlife are abundant in North America. Some animal populations have even exploded in recent years, thanks to proper wildlife management. But human populations have also expanded, and that is why we must face many wildlife dilemmas. We have needs and so do the animals. It is fortunate that we can learn to cope with wildlife through books such as this but unfortunate that the animals do not have the same capabilities. The animals that share our backyards can only accept that we are here and adjust accordingly by following their instincts.

A few chapters in this book provide the necessary information you will need to discover wildlife living near you. You will learn their habits and how their unpredictable activities can affect you. You will also see tracks of some creatures to help you identify those that utilize your land and backyard. When faced with a nuisance animal, such as those that dine in the flower patch, raid our trash cans, kill our pets and livestock, or take human lives, you may discover how to cope with their misbehavior and/or prevent a recurrence. However, I do not leave out mentions of some of the gruesome stories that have developed in recent years involving man and animal. Animal attacks on humans have occurred close to home, and they will likely continue, simply because many people have little knowledge about the animals surrounding them. To say the least, humans have lost touch with nature in our civilized world. The beaver, black bear, coyote, fox, mountain lion, rabbit, raccoon, squirrel, and white-tailed deer are but a few of the animals included in this book.

In the early chapters, you will learn everything you need to know about dealing with a problem animal including whom to call. You will also learn how to take matters into your own hands. Additionally, you will find several tables in the book. Several states contributed statistics that show the number of complaints connected with different species and the kinds of problems they cause.

I have also provided information about diseases, some of which affect the animal's health and some that can be transmitted to humans by animals. In addition, you will learn how to create wildlife habitat and what our officials have done to better manage wildlife. For the average individual, education is the key. The more you understand about wildlife, the fewer problems you will encounter and the more you will enjoy the presence of mammals. You can then pass along this education to your children, who will manage the wildlife of tomorrow. This book will provide the necessary information to make you more knowledgeable and, perhaps, a wildlife educator.

Most people will not sit down and read every word of this book. Often you will just want to seek information about a particular species. Each chapter that deals with a particular species is categorized, such as, birds, carnivores, hoofed mammals, etc. But I do urge you to read the early chapters, simply because they will give you a better understanding about any animal. These chapters will also provide valuable insight for coping with a nuisance animal. Finally, the beginning chapters may offer a better future for all wildlife near our homes.

I seriously doubt that you will find the contents of this book anywhere else. After all, we have just reached a point where man and animal living side-by-side have become so important. It has been building steam for several decades but action is now imperative. I salute our wildlife officials and qualified biologists in North America for the fine job they have done of managing wildlife. However, people in the suburbs, rural areas, and urban districts must also comply. I believe this book will help every reader accomplish that desirable end.

CHAPTER 1

Sharing Land with Wildlife

As we continue to expand into undeveloped lands, whether it be for commercial, industrial or residential purposes, we increasingly find ourselves sharing land with wildlife. Many species of animals, however, have found that they cannot retreat. They must share our surroundings and adjust to our habitat if they are to survive. These same animals often become nuisances whose actions are intolerable. There are ranchers who dread looking at their flock the next morning in fear they will see the blood and remains of a sheep that coyotes brutally killed the night before. Then there are farmers who must look at an entire section of soybeans that became a tasty meal for hungry woodchucks or white-tailed deer. Or how about the homeowner such as myself who must take a count of chickens and turkeys each day to see what the fox ate, or the woman next door who will step outside to see her room-sized garden devoured by an unknown animal? I could go on and on, but you get the point.

Now don't get me wrong. I do not blame these actions on wildlife, nor do I want to see our nuisance animals vanish to make more room for the people. I see wild animals about 300 days a

year and enjoy, well, almost every minute. However, in our changing society and developing world, we have found that problems
associated with animals have drastically increased in recent decades. Now we must come to understand the problems if we hope
to find the solutions. For many folks that have little understanding
of wildlife, that can be a most difficult task. First, we must take a
discerning look at why we have nuisance animals in every urban,
suburban and rural area today.

Animals have served a purpose in North America since the
earliest settlers. The people who built our first dirt roads and constructed our first towns relied heavily on wild game for food and
clothing. Actually, you could say it began before then, but these
explorers of our new continent were responsible for the boom in
homesteading and developing, after reporting an abundance of wildlife in a vast wilderness that you and I call home today. When man
shared land with wildlife in these early times, he was considered
the stranger.

Today, however, much has changed. Make no mistake, we
still share this beautiful land with wildlife, and most of us still greatly
enjoy their company. But nearly every animal species in North
America must now move aside to make room for the human race.
It did not happen overnight, but it did seem to come all too quickly.

Statistics tell us that approximately three people are born in
this world every second. Now I do not know how many that trans-
lates to throughout the U.S. and Canada, but I do know that our
populations have increased significantly in the last few decades.
From 1950 to 1990, the U.S. population has gone up 75 percent,
and over the same four decades Canada's population has nearly
doubled. Currently, our populations are at the levels of double-
figure millions in Canada and the triple-figure millions in the U.S.

You must also consider that these millions of people need
resources. There is electricity and power lines, oil, gas, and coal,
and their generation or acquisition destroys wildlife habitat.
Similarly, paper and paperboard use is vital to our growing

populations but often detrimental to wildlife. In fact, according to a 1989 data base, the U.S. relies more on paper and paperboard than many countries combined.

I am not against timber cutting, but it is a bit overdone in many portions of North America. In some localities strict regulations apply to timber cutting for the benefit of both man and wildlife. But in other areas where few regulations exist, timber cutting can be the sole reason why many species of wildlife must come into our backyards. Of course, not all animals require vast, dense forests. Some will flourish in the new openings created as a result of timber cutting, simply because they need this type of habitat. Others, though, require resources that we consistently remove. We have problems today with nuisance animals because of their habitat loss or because their only available habitat bumps up against our cities and suburbs.

Development is the primary reason for the major loss of wildlife habitat, and it destroys thousands of acres each day in North America. Our numerous roads are a perfect example, yet we continue cutting away habitat so that we can get from Point A to Point B a few minutes quicker. It seems we can do little to stop this growth, though many environmentalists do claim that we would be far better off repairing the old roads. But we can attempt to make better habitat along our roadways, according to some officials. Approximately 50 million acres have been lost to highways in the United States. Many states have recognized these astonishing figures and have responded by planting more wildlife habitat along our roadsides.

Roads also kill a large number of animals each day. In some states deer/vehicle collisions have just about caused the insurance companies to hit the panic stage. Of course, we feel this pinch whenever we pay our premiums. Each year, hundreds of thousands of deer die on our highways, even though wildlife officials increase hunter harvests annually in some states/provinces with the intention of reducing herds.

According to one study, more than 700,000 deer/vehicle collisions occurred on U.S. roads in 1991, resulting in more than $1 billion in damages.

Shortly after preparation begun on this book, I traveled Illinois SR 394 from the suburbs of Chicago. In a 15-mile stretch that began just south of I-80, my wife and I counted 5 deer, 2 raccoons, 1 coyote and 1 red fox, all of which had become highway fatalities. Road kills are so common, in fact, that many state officials estimate the rise and fall of animal populations of some species in a given area by taking counts of the dead. This method has provided many of our game departments with fairly accurate estimates, thus enabling them to regulate harvests annually.

According to the Virginia Department of Transportation, approximately $3.7 million in property damage resulted from deer/vehicle collisions in 1987. Sadly, more than 200 people were injured in these accidents. A survey conducted by Cornell University in 1988 showed between 38,000 to 57,000 deer/vehicle accidents occur in New York each year.

On a larger scale, another interesting study claimed that 726,000 deer/vehicle collisions occurred in the United States in 1991. The survey also noted that the average vehicle repair bill as a result of those accidents was $1,577. If one multiplied that with the 726,000 reported collisions, they will come up with about $1.1 billion. Equally disheartening is knowing that 90 percent or more of the deer struck by vehicles die.

Enough said about roads. The biggest reason that many animals become a nuisance, and the primary reason that their habitat is lost, comes from suburbanization and the clearing of lands, whether it be for agricultural farming, or industrial, commercial and residential developers.

Suburbanization simply means that our urban areas expand into the rural areas. In recent years, city folks have gotten the burning desire to live in the country. Many have gone that extra step by selling their urban home and moving into the country after buying a chunk of land. Each day, more and more large parcels of land are broken into smaller ones. Here's how it works. The landowner who had 500 acres suddenly sells the large tract of land to a developer who breaks it up into small segments of only a few acres or less that sells it to all the folks that want a piece of the country. Unfortunately, though, many of these individuals know little about wildlife. As one wildlife official put it, "These people then become the stewards of wildlife without any training."

I can understand the thoughts of those that yearn to wake up every morning in the country. After all, I have enjoyed this kind of living for many years and wouldn't trade it for a lifetime supply of mom's homemade donuts. These individuals simply have that craving to get close to nature. Many have the idea that they will be encompassed by wildlife, viewing it day after day. However, nothing is further from the truth. We seldom see most nocturnal wild animals, and only occasionally do we have the opportunity to view wild diurnal animals.

No doubt, though, people do have quite an interest in wildlife. According to a survey conducted by the U.S. Fish and Wildlife Service in 1985, 74 percent of the U.S. population 16 years old and over participated in some form of wildlife viewing, feeding or photography as a primary or secondary recreational activity. This was an increase of 20 percent compared to the same study done in the 1980s. They also noted that 16 percent of the U.S. population, 16 years old and over, took trips for the sole purpose of observing, photographing or feeding wildlife. More than 25 percent of this group took trips outside their state of residence. The total spent on trip-related expenditures for their wildlife activities exceeded $4 billion.

When I was a youngster, I can remember going out the front door of my city home and walking less than one-half mile to get into the country. Many walking trails interlaced the old thickets and timber in this somewhat wild country that butted up against the city limits where one could still hear the busy world not too far away. But I treasured these moments, and the retreat that made them possible, simply because I could escape into a world far beyond what many of us call reality. Before I moved away from the city, however, the retreat gave way to bulldozers and became just another shopping center and residential area in a small portion of a growing town. Today, I would assume that another youngster lives on the edge of what was once my retreat, and is walking to his refuge each time he needs to get close to nature.

Sooner or later, we will run out of retreats. One subdivision expands into the rural areas, and the suburbs soon become cities. In the process, our precious wildlife must share our habitat when there is no place left to move aside. Ernie Provost, a professor of wildlife biology at the University of Georgia, hit the nail on the head when he chose who to blame for the loss of wildlife habitat.

"For years and years I told my students that the primary problem facing wildlife management was the loss of wildlife habitat. The second problem was people," explained Provost. Pausing for a moment, Provost said, "Well, I was wrong. The number one problem is people. If it were not for the people, we wouldn't have the habitat problem."

Provost added that we must all learn to understand wildlife

and assume responsibility for the actions of animals that must share their space with the people who move into their domain. He wonders how we can blame the coyote that eats the puppy or the fox that raids the chicken house.

The loss of wetlands has also contributed to diminishing wildlife habitat. And in case you did not know, our wetlands do much more than provide homes for much of North America's wildlife. Wetlands purify polluted waters, check the destructive power of floods and storms, and provide recreational activities for many people each year. Wetlands include a variety of wet environments — from coastal and inland marshes to bottomlands, mudflats and ponds. However, more than 100 million acres of the original wetlands of the United States have been destroyed. From the mid-1950s to the mid-1970s, such losses averaged 458,000 acres a year. Surprisingly, an estimated 54 percent of the wetlands that existed in colonial times have vanished forever, with many states in the

Our wetlands provide homes for many species of wildlife. Unfortunately, we have lost millions of acres of valuable wetlands in recent decades, putting some species of wildlife out of business.

State	Percent Lost
California	91
Illinois	85
Indiana	87
Iowa	89
Kentucky	81
Missouri	87
Ohio	90

Table 1. States that have lost more than 75 percent of their wetlands between the 1780s and mid-1980s. At least 15 additional states not shown here have lost more than 50 percent of their wetlands since the colonial times. Source: U.S. Fish and Wildlife Service.

Midwest suffering the most losses (Table 1).

The amount of space needed by a particular species of wildlife varies. The chipmunk, for example, can live in a very small area, perhaps no more than one-half acre. The mountain lion and grizzly bear, though, will need several square miles of habitat. The white-tailed deer and the wild turkey may spend their entire life in two square miles or less, providing food and proper habitat exists. Take away any wild animal's food and habitat, however, and there are sure to be problems. Many animals are now on the endangered and/or protected list simply because these necessary ingredients vanished. On the other hand, many species of wildlife still remain as their habitat slowly disappears, moving on until they find more. Then there are those animals that become troublesome pests only when their food supply dwindles. This theory applies to many normally timid animals, such as the black bear and mountain lion, which may suddenly appear out of nowhere when their natural foods become unavailable.

People in many states and provinces that have high densities of black bear seldom see the mysterious, shy animals until they get hungry. Once this occurs, the bears begin showing up in the suburbs and cities looking for something to eat. Sometimes that something turns out to be a garbage can full or goodies, but many times it can be John Doe's pet dog or cat.

Most of our nuisance animals, however, are not close to the endangered list. For instance, in the early 1900s there were fewer than 500,000 white-tailed deer in North America. My latest find-ings indicate there are now about 20 million deer roaming in the United States and Canada. Each year, state and province officials increase annual bag limits in areas where deer populations need reducing. Despite these actions, the white-tailed deer continues to flourish. These animals are adaptable to various types of habitat and have proved that they will thrive and multiply in most any area that man has invaded.

The return of the wild turkey is another unbelievable story. Due to habitat destruction and poaching in the early to mid-1900s, this magnificent game bird was nearly obliterated from the United States. However, in recent decades the work of sportsmen, wild-life professionals, the National Wild Turkey Federation and other concerned organizations has brought back the birds, introducing them into many areas where turkeys may have never existed. One example occurred in Ontario a few years ago when the province traded moose to Michigan for wild turkeys. Approximately 4,200,000 wild turkeys currently inhabit North America (that num-ber has increased since this was written), occupying about 800,000 square miles.

There were fewer than 100,000 elk in 1900. Today, about a million wapiti call North America their home as they continue to expand in areas where they have always been found, as well as in many new areas. In fact, only a few months before this book be-gan, 23 elk made a 5,000-mile journey from Alberta to a vast area of hardwoods called Land Between the Lakes (LBL) in Kentucky and Tennessee. Elk inhabited LBL more than 150 years ago, but everyone now hopes that the wapiti herd will once again become permanent residents of the area.

In the following chapters you will read about many species of wildlife that have become nuisance animals, where they are stir-ring up trouble, and find the remedies for dealing with them. I also urge you to read about the animal habits so that you will understand precisely what makes them tick. While doing so, keep in mind that our wildlife is truly a spiritual boost for all of us. We need them as much as they need us. Finally, we must also realize that as long as we keep expanding onto their turf, there will be conflicts between man and animal.

CHAPTER 2

Nuisance Animals — Statiscally Speaking

Once preparation of this book got underway, I began extensive research on the subject of nuisance animals. I had previously jotted down notes after talking with various individuals and wildlife officials, thinking I had heard about every imaginable story involving problems between wildlife and people. I had also kept records of personal occurrences, realizing that there is a major problem facing the people and wildlife of North America today. However, after the research data came pouring in, it became obvious that I had, at best, only scraped the surface. It also became apparent that nuisance animals are more than just a problem. They cost taxpayers millions of dollars each year and have caused damage that has resulted in loss of human productivity, property and lives.

My research included questions that I presented to officials in states/provinces, and various departments in the U.S. and Canada. My goal was to see exactly what animal species caused the most problems and where the damage primarily occurred. I also hoped to gain an insight on the types of complaints that were the most common.

Throughout this chapter you will see nuisance animal statistics from various states and provinces. You will also see information that was provided by the U.S. Department of Agriculture (USDA), Animal and Plant Health Inspection Service (APHIS) and Animal Damage Control (ADC). Some states/provinces do not keep detailed records of complaints and damages caused by wildlife, while others keep in-depth reports. For example, one may record only the total number of complaints while another keeps precise records of animal species that cause problems, a description of the type of damage and how the matter was resolved. Exact total numbers of nuisance animals do not exist on the national level either. However, a study here and there, along with estimates, does give us a clearer picture of the problems that exist between man and wildlife today.

The information that follows in the pages ahead is quite interesting. I think anyone that has encountered nuisance wildlife, whether that animal be a squirrel that has set up a temporary home in the chimney, or a carnivore that ran off with the baby ducks, will find that they are not alone.

Each year, the state of Illinois issues nuisance animal removal permits to landowners or tenants if officials confirm existence of damage and have no other effective alternatives for resolving the matter. Thus, permittees can provide nuisance animal management services for other people. In 1994, the permittees handled no less than 45,000 nuisance animals. It is not surprising, however, that nuisance animals caused far more problems than they did in 1993 (Table 2). Overall, the number of complaints reported by permittees increased 11.4 percent from 1993 to 1994. Most complaints (83.3 percent) were reported by permittees working in Region II. Interestingly, Region II includes the Chicago area.

Officials of the Illinois nuisance wildlife management program say that conflicts between humans and animals are likely to increase in the state because of (1) urban expansion, (2) increasing populations of many furbearing animals, (3) reduced fur harvests associated with low pelt values and (4) gradual improvements of

urban habitats for rac-
coons and squirrels as a
result of maturation of
trees in areas developed
on agricultural lands during the 1950s and 1960s.
The rising trend of nui-
sance animal complaints
should support these four
factors.

Species	Total	Percent Change
Beaver	1,737	+ 17.2
Coyote	317	+ 24.3
Fox	81	+ 55.8
Muskrat	3,189	+ 21.7
Opossum	4,539	- 2.2
Raccoon	13,193	+ 13.4
Squirrel	8,591	+ 15.5
Striped Skunk	3,641	+ 43.5
Woodchuck	4,154	+ 10.6

Table 2. Numbers of some species handled by
Nuisance Wildlife Control Permittees in Illinois,
1994, and changes from previous year. Bats,
birds, chipmunks and deer accounted for many
more animal complaints. Source: Illinois
Department of Conservation.

Although the small
state of Rhode Island re-
ported only 437 nuisance
animal complaints in
1995 (Table 3), the types
of species ranged from
ospreys to otters. A tally from the Division of Fish, Wildlife and
Estuarine Resources showed a variety of types of complaints. Rabbits were eating garden vegetables in some areas, while in another
location a coyote had simply entered into someone's backyard where
its appearance was not appreciated. Bats also set up in or near
homes while a few ducks and geese had made a mess in the yards
of some folks. Elsewhere squirrels chewed on electrical wires and,
more seriously, raccoons were suspected to be carrying rabies.

New Hampshire Fish and Game and ADC entered into a
funded cooperative agreement to address wildlife damage problems in 1986 with the intention of providing professional respon-
sive assistance to citizens in the state. According to a recent report, the program has directly responded to about 1,500 requests
for assistance each year from a variety of wildlife damage problems. However, they recently surpassed that figure after receiving
more than 2,200 complaints. Officials claim the increase is related
to public concern over the mid-Atlantic strain of rabies in raccoons
that entered the state in 1992. There have also been significant

Species	Total
Beaver	12
Bobcat	4
Canada Geese	67
Coyote	21
Deer	45
Fox	4
Hawk	3
Muskrat	3
Opossum	7
Otter	9
Raccoon	26
Skunk	15
Snakes	22
Squirrel	30
Wolf	4
Woodchuck	15

Table 3. Numbers of some species that Rhode Island had complaints about in 1995. Source: Rhode Island Dept. of Environmental Management.

increases in bear problems and the need of assistance from citizens to help them cope with bears in recent years.

Raccoons, bears, skunks, squirrels, woodchucks, beavers and deer accounted for about 70 percent of the problems reported in New Hampshire in 1994. When citizens have problems with these species, they usually request assistance since it often involves human health and safety, or property damage in residential settings. The black bear and white-tailed deer accounted for about 24 percent of the problems, while raccoons were responsible for 19 percent of the complaints received.

South Dakota's ADC office reported 4,604 resource incidents that resulted in agricultural and property damage from nuisance animals in 1995 (Table 4). Coyote complaints totaled 2,169 and were primarily responsible for some form of livestock (agriculture) damage. There were at least 1,487 cases of coyotes attacking sheep and 418 domestic turkeys that became victims of the wily coyote. The total loss as a result of this agriculture damage surpassed $150,000. Feral dogs also accounted for 45 attacks on sheep.

Property damage incidents totaled 229 with a total loss value of about $50,000. Beavers were responsible for 167 complaints and their damage alone totaled $41,750. The total value of agricultural and property damage in South Dakota exceeded $275,000.

Each year, Kentucky does a statewide wildlife management survey to obtain data on problem animal species, the kinds of damage they cause, and how to initiate the proper control procedures. The Wildlife Damage Survey sends complaint forms to conservation officers and wildlife personnel to obtain the necessary data.

Species	Incidents	Loss
Badger	17	$1,975
Beaver	1,739	$113,617
Bobcat	5	$45
Coyote	2,169	$152,642
Dogs, Feral	45	$2,555
Eagle, Golden	5	$600
Fox	99	$950
Mink	129	$1,120
Raccoon	380	$10,768

The latest survey showed that 914 reports of wildlife/human conflicts were received during 1994. This was the highest number of incidents received since Kentucky began the survey in 1982, and it constituted a 65 percent increase from 1993. However, this was largely due to the 60 percent increase in the number of deer damage complaints from the previous

Table 4. Agriculture and property resource losses in South Dakota resulting from nuisance animals during 1995. Source: South Dakota Animal Damage Control.

year. Officials claim that deer complaints have been the primary factor influencing the trend in nuisance animals for all species combined since 1982.

Kentucky deer complaint reports totaled 711, raccoons 53, muskrats 22, and beavers 18. These five species accounted for more than 80 percent of the total number of complaints received in 1994. Kentucky's small population of black bears caused three incidents, while various other species also caused some problems.

According to the Wildlife Damage Survey, the rising number of complaints rose to a record high in 1994 for several species because of higher densities of some animals, thus increasing human/wildlife conflicts. Officials also noted that there may be a decreasing tolerance level of wildlife by landowners.

By 1990, the Wisconsin Department of Natural Resources had decided that field personnel were spending an inordinate amount of time responding to nuisance wildlife complaints from the public. They received 1,043 requests for assistance that year, including the trapping and relocating of 381 black bears. This soon led to a cooperative agreement with the USDA and ADC.

Today, one can understand why Wisconsin officials received additional assistance. In 1995, there were more than 9,000 requests for assistance received from the public regarding nuisance animals. That is nearly twice the number of complaints received in 1992 and several times more than the total number received in 1990.

Most of the incidents in 1995 came from individuals who complained of problems with fowl. Species of birds that became nuisances in Wisconsin included blackbirds, coots, crows, eagles, geese, gulls, hawks, owls, pigeons, wild turkeys and many others. As for the owls, the great horned owl received 30 complaints, while barn owls received only two complaints. However, when it comes to both small and large nuisance mammals, Wisconsin has certainly had its share (Table 5). Raccoons and black bear led the way totaling more than 2,800 complaints, while white-tailed deer, skunks and marmots/woodchucks were responsible for 2,440. I'm not sure how or why, but at least one complaint came in on frogs/toads.

Raccoons have apparently done a good job of harassing Michigan citizens in recent years, too. According to reports from the

Species	Complaints
Badger	225
Beaver	385
Black Bear	1,478
Bobcat	18
Cat, Feral	26
Coyote	140
Deer	931
Dog, Feral	32
Ducks	88
Fisher	18
Fox	77
Geese	290
Marmot, Woodchuck	663
Mink	10
Muskrat	118
Opossum	131
Porcupine	51
Rabbit	134
Raccoon	1,385
Skunk	846
Squirrel	555
Wolves	20

Table 5. Nuisance animal complaints received in 1995 of some Wisconsin species. Source: Wisconsin Department of Natural Resources.

wildlife division, more raccoons caused problems from 1992 to 1994 than any other small mammal. During the three-year period, the Wildlife Division received 14,049 complaints about raccoons. I might add, this is an apparent trend that has occurred in other states.

Table 6 shows that complaints on at least six other species — bats, beavers, coyotes, opossums, skunks and woodchucks — have also shown astonishing increases in Michigan. Feral pigeons (not shown in the table) have also become a nightmare for many residents. Complaints on feral pigeons nearly tripled in the three years. Many other species such as gophers, muskrats, rabbits and squirrels have also seen their numbers of complaints rise since 1992.

Urban folks seldom face the same wildlife problems that people encounter in the suburbs and rural areas, and rarely do urban residents contend with the same species. However, those who live in urban districts do have their share of animal complaints and, in some cases, suffer from wildlife damage. That may have been proven in a mail questionnaire that was sent to all Extension Wildlife Specialists, or persons in similar positions who explored topics related to urban wildlife damage for a portion of 1986 and 1987.

According to an article by Wayne R. Marion, a manager of

Species	1992 Complaints	1993 Complaints	1994 Complaints	Total Complaints
Bats	613	993	1,087	2,693
Beaver	149	293	368	810
Coyote	22	42	59	123
Opossum	930	992	1,198	3,120
Raccoon	4,221	4,418	5,410	14,049
Skunk	1,551	1,668	2,444	5,663
Woodchuck	1,106	1,670	1,887	4,663

Table 6. From 1992 to 1994, increasing trends of some nuisance animals indicate more problems ahead for Michigan wildlife officials. Source: Michigan Department of Natural Resources.

wildlife resources, the response to the urban wildlife damage questionnaire was excellent. Although the specialists identified 25 categories of vertebrates that were problem species they often had to provide information of when urban people asked, bats were the most frequently mentioned. Snakes were second while tree squirrels were the third most frequent species for urban residents. Several types of roosting birds caused problems, as did striped skunks, raccoons and rats/mice. Marion stated, however, that bats and snakes were not always the real troublemakers.

"It is interesting to note that two groups of animals normally feared by people, bats and snakes, are right at the top of the list in terms of request for information but they rank considerably lower when actual damage is involved," said Marion.

Marion also explained that certain species of wildlife just happen to be in the wrong place at the wrong time, such as a woodpecker hammering away at a downspout or a pigeon roosting on a structure. "Then there are those species that fit into the actual damage category (e.g., moles in the yard, pocket gophers in the field). And finally, there seems to be a whole cadre of species, such as bats, snakes, scorpions and alligators that seem to evoke a fear in people that is not really warranted based upon the actual number of attacks or real threats to human health and livelihood. These fears seem to be deeply ingrained in us through our culture as fears of the unknown."

Marion claimed that values of damage caused by urban wildlife was difficult to estimate for various reasons, but it came down to these figures: White-tailed deer ($30.6 million), pocket gophers ($5.2 million), rats/mice ($2.7 million), tree squirrels ($2.0 million), and roosting birds ($2.0 million). Other species that were estimated to have caused $1 million in damage or less were, in frequency of damage, woodpeckers, raccoons, armadillos, bats, moles and rabbits.

For many years, the Missouri Department of Conservation has provided technical advice and specialized materials (at cost) to property owners who reported nuisance animals. For complaints received in 1991 and 1992, complainants were asked to complete a mail survey that would provide data such as the type, location and extent of damage, resolution of the problem information, and if the property owner was satisfied with the program for dealing with nuisance animals as practiced by the department.

The survey indicated that 22 wildlife species caused damage, with coyotes (53 percent), beavers (25 percent) and white-tailed deer (18 percent) created the most problems for complainants. Rural areas received 94 percent of the damage caused while 48 percent

Species	Primary Complaint	Secondary Complaint
Armadillo	General presence	Rooting up yards/fields
Bats	Presence, noise and odor	
Bear	In garbage	Livestock loss, damage to bee hives and orchards
Beaver	Tree cutting, crop and boat dock damage	Plugging drain pipes, burrowing
Coyote	Occasional poultry loss	Concern of future poultry/livestock loss
Deer	Garden damage, broken fences	Antler rub damage to orchards
Fox	Living under houses	Occasional poultry loss
Muskrat	General presence	Burrowing in dams, damage to boat docks
Opossum	General presence	Poultry loss
Otter	Occasional fish loss	Frequent fish loss
Rabbit	Garden damage	Truck patch on farming, orchards
Skunk	Presence in buildings	Digging in turf
Waterfowl	Field crops	General nuisance
Woodchuck	Garden damage, burrowing	Row crop

Table 7. Primary and secondary causes of complaints about some nuisance animals. Source: Missouri Department of Conservation.

occurred to livestock, followed by property damage (27 percent) and crop damage (13 percent).

The types of damage caused by Missouri wildlife species varied, but as Table 7 indicates, many animals seemed to stick to one bad habit. I have provided only the primary and secondary types of complaints in the table. However, more than one complaint may occur in either bracket. I should add, many species received several types of complaints. For instance, the coyote was caught eating watermelons that did not belong to him, while the skunk has been turned in to officials because of an odor problem.

Investigating animal damage requires many hours that can result in major costs to wildlife agencies on the local and national levels. Every hour spent traveling to and from a site, every hour necessary to make a full investigation, adds costs. Annually these may exceed thousands or millions of dollars in time alone. A summary of Nova Scotia's 1993 Wildlife Investigation Report shows that more than 8,000 hours were used by personnel investigating wildlife problems. The problems ranged from nuisance animals and distressed wildlife to sightings that also had to be investigated. In addition, personnel drove about 220,000 kilometers to look into the complaints. Nuisance reports of only big game animals (bear, deer and moose) required more than 500 staff hours and 14,000 kilometers driven to investigate the problems (Table 8).

Species	Kilometers Driven	Investigation Hours
Bear	12,264	452.72
Deer	2,430	106.69
Moose	285	8.92
Total	14,979	568.33

Table 8. Number of Nova Scotia wildlife nuisance reports for big game species, kilometers driven and hours spent investigating in 1993. Source: Nova Scotia Department of Natural Resources.

Montana sheep and lamb producers lost 92,000 livestock animals (a value of $5.3 million) to weather, disease, predators and other causes during 1995, according to a survey conducted by the Montana Agricultural Statistics Service. Predators caused approximately $2 million in losses in 1995, up from

$1.9 million the previous year (Table 9).

Coyotes kill more sheep and lambs than any other predator. The value of losses attributed to coyotes was $1.5 million, and the number of sheep and lambs lost to all predators totaled 37,100 head. However, this was nearly 5,000 fewer than the total number of

Predator	Number of Losses	Value of Losses
Fox	3,400	$166,100
Dog	1,600	$101,400
Coyote	28,000	$1,513,400
Eagle	2,700	$138,500
Bear	300	$18,000
Mountain Lion	500	$31,100
Unknown Predators	600	$32,600
Total Predator Losses	37,100	$2,001,000

Table 9. Montana sheep and lamb losses by predators in 1995. Source: Montana Agricultural Statistics Service.

sheep/lambs lost in 1994. Coyotes killed 500 fewer sheep, and foxes killed 2,600 less than they did in 1995. Eagles also killed 2,700 sheep/lambs in 1995, compared to 5,300 in 1994. Non-predatory losses totaled $2.8 million in 1995 and accounted for 51 percent of all sheep/lamb losses.

Sheep and lamb losses are not limited to Montana, however. In fact, during 1994 predators managed to kill a whopping 368,050 sheep and lambs in the United States. According to a report published by the USDA's Agricultural Statistics Service, coyotes were again the major cause of losses with 66.2 percent of the total predator losses in 1994 (Table 10). Surprisingly, dogs were second in terms of causing losses.

Coyotes were also the major predator of goats in the five major producing states (Arizona, Michigan, New Mexico, Oklahoma and

Predator	Total Head Lost	Percent of Total Predators	Value
Bears	12,250	3.3	$640,150
Bobcats	9,200	2.5	$418,425
Coyotes	243,800	66.2	$11,504,900
Dogs	40,325	11.0	$2,206,975
Eagles	15,000	4.1	$641,150
Foxes	12,350	3.4	$507,250
Mountain Lions	28,500	7.7	$1,460,600
Others	6,625	1.8	$337,450
Total U.S. Losses	368,050	100.0	$17,716,900

Table 10. Losses of sheep and lambs from predators in the United States during 1994. Source: USDA National Agricultural Statistics Service.

Texas). The value of goats lost from all predators totaled $5.48 million in 1994.

As for regional statistics, the area named Mountain and West accounted for the highest sheep/lamb losses from coyotes with a reported $10.5 million. The Midwest area suffered losses in excess of $418,000, while the South and East region showed a loss of about $600,000.

The National Agricultural Statistics Service also reported that more than one-half of United States farms surveyed in 1989 suffered losses caused by wildlife during a 12-month period (Table 11). The species category most frequently reported as a cause of damage was "Hoofed Animals" (antelope, deer, elk, javelina, wild horses, burros and hogs). Carnivores that are primarily flesh eaters, such as coyote, fox, raccoon and others, were responsible for 22 percent of the farm losses.

The survey was sent to a randomly selected 20,000 farms and ranches to assess the incidence of losses to agriculture by wildlife. The types of agriculture was categorized by products — Livestock, Field Crops, Fruits/Vegetables/Nuts, Other and All Species. Those farms and ranches in the Fruit/Vegetables/Nuts category

suffered the most losses but close behind were those in the Livestock and Field Crops categories.

In 1993, a report from the USDA to show the damage to corn
by wildlife in the 10 largest corn producing states revealed that
less than one percent of corn for grain, 35.4 million bushels, was
lost to wildlife. The 10 states account for over 80 percent of the
U.S. corn production, and harvested 5.14 billion bushels in 1993.
On a per acre basis, 0.70 bushels (39 pounds) were lost to wildlife
across the 10 states. Birds caused a loss of about 10 million bushels of corn for grain, while deer caused slightly more damage for a
loss of 12 million bushels.

The USDA also reported that predators during 1995 killed

Table 11. Percent of farms/ranches experiencing loss due to animal damage by
region and type of species in the United States from August 1, 1988 through
July 31, 1989 (multiple occurrences counted only once). Source: USDA,
National Agricultural Statistics Service.

Species Category	Northeast Region	Southeast Region	North-Central Region	West Region	United States
Birds	10.8	11.2	9.3	13.3	10.6
Carnivores	24.1	20.7	20.6	22.2	21.7
Hoofed Mammals	37.7	20.4	41.4	15.9	33.4
Rodents/Rabbits	30.2	18.6	27.5	23.1	26.3
Others	3.2	8.7	4.0	5.9	4.6
All Species	57.8	47.5	57.5	49.1	54.9

STATES BY REGION:

Northeast: CT, DE, KY, ME, MD, MA, NH, NJ, NY, NC, PA, TN, RI, VT,
VA, WV
Southeast: AL, AR, FL, GA, LA, MS, SC
North-Central: IL, IN, IA, KS, MI, MN, MO, NE, ND, OH, SD, WI
West: AK, AZ, CA, CO, HI, ID, MT, NV, NM, OK, OR, TX, UT, WA, WY

117,400 cattle in the United States (excluding Alaska). These losses cost farmers and ranchers a total of $39.6 million. Again, coyotes were the number one culprit, being responsible for 55 percent of the total predatory kills. Dogs accounted for another 17.6 percent of the cattle loss, while bears, mountain lions, wolves and other animals were responsible for the remainder.

In 1993, the Minnesota Department of Natural Resources conducted a national study to determine facts about the wildlife damage control programs in other states. A questionnaire was sent to 50 state wildlife agencies to get an assessment of the primary wildlife damage problems, species responsible for problems, agency responsibilities, sources of funds and costs for programs, and types of assistance they offered.

Of noteworthy interest and value on the questionnaire were each state's answers to the most frequent wildlife species damage complaints (Table 12). Although Minnesota's questionnaire asked each state to include five species in order of their frequency of complaints, I have provided only the first four. A total of 43 states responded to the questionnaire.

Not surprisingly, 19 states named deer and one state (Montana) claimed mule deer as their primary species of wildlife causing damage. Only one state (Colorado) showed elk as the primary species. Next in line was the raccoon, as seven states reported the masked bandit as the primary cause of damage. Two states claimed the black bear, while three each claimed that coyotes (one state listed predators) and beavers were the primary cause.

When it comes to those species causing economic damage, at least 23 states reported that deer had cost the most. Elk were listed as the highest cost in economic damage in four states, while beavers ranked at the top on six occasions.

The Minnesota survey also asked each state to identify their three major predators and their primary causes of damage in descending order of significance. Table 13 shows the three predators (some states claim only one or two predators causing damage) and

Table 12. Wildlife species damage complaints in order of frequency, as reported by 43 states. Survey compiled by Minnesota Dept. of Natural Resources in cooperation with the Minnesota Dept. of Agriculture.

State	First	Second	Third	Fourth
AK	Black Bear	Grizzly Bear	Beaver	Moose
AL	Deer	Beaver	Cormorant	Coyote
AR	Beaver	Black Bird	Raccoon	Rodent
AZ	Coyote	Skunk	Javelina	Elk
CO	Elk	Deer	Black Bear	Cougar
CT	Raccoon	Squirrel	Beaver	Deer
DE	Deer	Goose	Woodchuck	Snake
FL	Predator	Beaver	Deer	Black Bear
GA	Deer	Raccoon	Beaver	Black Bear
HI	Feral Pig	Feral Sheep	Feral Goat	RV Bulbul
IA	Deer	Beaver	Goose	Raccoon
ID	Beaver	Deer	Elk	Goose
IL	Raccoon	Squirrel	Opossum	Skunk
KS	Gopher	Mole	Skunk	Deer
KY	Deer	Coyote	Muskrat	Raccoon
LA	Deer	Beaver	Black Bird	Wading Bird
MA	Raccoon	Squirrel	Woodchuck	Skunk
MD	Squirrel	Woodchuck	Black Bird	Deer
ME	Beaver	Coyote	Raccoon	Deer
MI	Deer	Raccoon	Goose	Beaver
MN	Deer	Beaver	Raccoon	Black Bear
MO	Deer	Raccoon	Squirrel	Beaver
MS	Deer	Beaver	Alligator	Raccoon
MT	Mule Deer	Elk	Coyote	Beaver
NC	Deer	Beaver	Woodpecker	Squirrel
NE	Coyote	Prairie Dog	Raccoon	Skunk
NH	Raccoon	Skunk	Squirrel	Woodchuck
NJ	Deer	Raccoon	Beaver	Black Bear
NM	Black Bear	Beaver	Elk	Cougar
NV	Ground Squirrel	Raccoon	Woodpecker	Cougar/Bear
NY	Raccoon	Beaver	Skunk	Squirrel
OH	Raccoon	Deer	Woodchuck	Squirrel
OR	Deer	Beaver	Raccoon	Elk
PA	Deer	Woodchuck	Rabbit	Beaver
RI	Raccoon	Squirrel	Woodchuck	Skunk
SC	Deer	Beaver	Squirrel	Raccoon
TN	Goose	Raccoon	Coyote	Beaver
TX	Coyote	Beaver	Deer	Squirrel
UT	Deer	Cougar	Black Bear	Raccoon
VA	Deer	Beaver	Bear	Goose
WI	Deer	Black Bear	Raccoon	Woodchuck
WV	Squirrel	Skunk	Raccoon	Deer
WY	Deer	Elk	Pronghorn	Moose

Table 13. Predators and damages in descending order of frequency as reported by 43 states. Survey compiled by Minnesota Dept. of Natural Resources in cooperation with the Minnesota Dept. of Agriculture.

State	Predator 1	Predator 2	Predator 3	Damage 1	Damage 2
AK	Grizzly Bear	Wolf		Reindeer	Dogs/Cats
AL	Coyote			Poultry	Cattle
AR	Coyote	Raccoon	Skunk	Poultry	Cattle
AZ	Coyote	Cougar	Black Bear	Cattle	Sheep
CO	Black Bear	Cougar		Cattle	Sheep
CT	Raccoon	Coyote		Sweet Corn	Sheep
DE	Fox	Raccoon		Poultry	
FL	Bobcat	Fox	Coyote	Poultry	Cattle
GA	Coyote	Fox	Bobcat	Watermelon	Hog
HI	Dog	Cat		Poultry	Sheep
IA	Coyote	Fox		Sheep	Hog
ID	Coyote	Black Bear	Cougar	Sheep	
IL	Raccoon	Opossum	Coyote	Dwellings	Dogs/Cats
KS	Coyote	Raccoon	Fox	Sheep	Cattle
KY	Dog	Coyote	Raptor	Cattle	Sheep
LA	Coyote	Wading Bird	Small Mammal	Aquaculture	Poultry
MA	Coyote	Fox	Otter	Sheep	Dogs/Cats
MD	Raccoon	Fox		Dwellings	Poultry
ME	Coyote	Black Bear		Sheep	Cattle
MI	Coyote	Fox		Sheep	Poultry
MN	Coyote	Wolf	Fox	Poultry	Sheep
MO	Coyote	Raccoon	Fox	Poultry	Sheep
MS	Coyote	Fox		Poultry	Cattle
MT	Coyote	Cougar	Black Bear	Sheep	Apiaries
NC	Fox	Raptor	Furbearers	Poultry	
NE	Coyote	Raccoon	Raptor	Sheep	Cattle
NH	Raccoon	Black Bear	Coyote	Nuisance	Sheep
NJ	Raccoon	Fox	Coyote	Poultry	Sheep
NM	Cougar	Black Bear	Coyote	Cattle	Sheep
NV	Cougar	Coyote	Black Bear	Sheep	Dogs/Cats
NY	Raccoon	Skunk	Coyote	Dwellings	Poultry
OH	Coyote	Raccoon		Sheep	Poultry
OR	Cougar	Coyote	Bobcat	Cattle	Sheep
PA	Raccoon	Fox	Coyote	Sweet Corn	Poultry
RI	Coyote	Fox		Dogs/Cats	Sheep
SC	Fox	Coyote		Poultry	
TN	Coyote	Raccoon	Skunk	Poultry	Cattle
TX	Coyote	Bobcat	Raccoon	Sheep	Poultry
UT	Coyote	Cougar	Black Bear	Sheep	Poultry
VA	Coyote	Bobcat		Cattle	Poultry
WI	Raptor	Wolf	Eagle	Poultry	Dogs/Cats
WV	Raccoon	Coyote	Weasel	Sheep	Row Crops
WY	Coyote	Cougar		Sheep	Horse

the first two causes of damage in order of their frequency.

No doubt, the coyote has gotten away with murder. In fact, at least 23 states claimed that their primary predator was the coyote. The raccoon came away with top honors in eight states, as did the fox. The cougar (mountain lion) was voted the number one predator by three states, and at least four states named it as their second choice.

If you raise chickens, guineas, turkeys or other poultry animals, you won't be happy to hear that poultry losses were the primary focal points of damage by predators in 13 states. The survey also showed that nine other states reported poultry as the second most significant sufferers from damage by predators. Thirteen states claimed that sheep were the predator's choice, while 12 states reported sheep as their second choice. Seven states rated cattle as the predator's main interest, and seven also claimed that cattle were their second choice.

The ADC addresses each reported occurrence of nuisance animals in one of four resource protection categories:

Agriculture includes livestock, feedlots, crops, fruits, vegetables, aquaculture, rangeland, timber, Christmas trees, or any other form of agricultural production.

Human Health and Safety includes safety hazards at airports, diseases that can be transmitted to man, and nuisances.

Property includes buildings, utilities, fences, dikes, dams, roads, irrigation structures, packaged and processed foods, turf, flowers, gardens, clothing, pets, equipment, machinery, ornamental plants and trees, or any other economic losses not included under the Agriculture category.

Natural Resources includes wildlife, sport fisheries, refuges, endangered species, parks and natural areas.

Resource losses of the four categories reported to the ADC during 1994 were in excess of $50 million (Figure 2-1).

Anyone, no matter where they live, may suffer from wildlife damage that falls into one or more of the four categories. Of

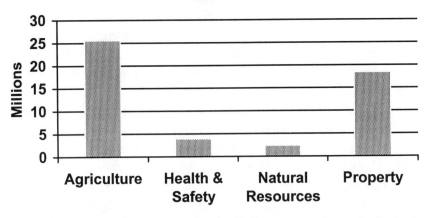

Figure 2.1. Resource losses reported to the ADC program as the result of animal damage exceeded $50 million in fiscal year 1994. Source: USDA, Animal Damage Control.

particular interest to many of us, though, are human injuries and deaths from wildlife bites and attacks. In the following chapters you will read about many of the human/animal confrontations, and the details of the species and individual involved. However, an article published by the *Wildlife Society Bulletin 1995* titled "Review of human injuries, illnesses, and economical losses caused by wildlife in the United States," showed that an average of 4,203 rodent, 76 fox and 113 skunk bites were reported annually in 15 states studied. All bites proved to be non-fatal. Black bear, grizzly bear, mountain lion, coyotes, American alligators and venomous snakes were also responsible for some bites and attacks, but their totals do not compare with rodents, fox and skunk bites. Based on populations in the 15-state area in the study, there were 10.6 rodent, 0.2 fox, and 0.3 skunk bites per 100,000 people. The article concluded that rattlesnakes are responsible for about 6,000 to 8,000 venomous snake bites annually in the U.S. and account for most fatalities, many of which were to people that deliberately handle snakes. The article also indicated that about 35,000 people are bitten in the U.S. annually by wildlife, but fatalities average only 10 to 16 each year. From the study, one could estimate that 26,700 people will be bitten by rodents, 500 by foxes and 750 by skunks annually.

The article also showed a major economic loss to households as a result of wildlife, according to a survey done by Michael R. Conover. Over 1,000 households were randomly selected from the 100 largest metropolitan centers in the U.S. Half of those that responded to the survey (57 percent) reported that they or their households had a problem with a species of wildlife the previous year.

As mentioned near the beginning of this chapter, there are no national statistics/summaries available that will give us precise figures of animal damages, nuisance animal complaints, and economic damage. But speculation suggests that the economic losses from wildlife complaints and damage alone may get into the billions of dollars lost each year. However, throughout this chapter I have provided you with information that will give you some idea of the primary species that cause problems in both urban and rural areas, the various types of damage caused and the extent of the damages in economic values. The exact numbers of nuisance animals, though, are much, much higher than those reported in this chapter. Some states and provinces do not keep accurate records of nuisance animal complaints or the damage they cause, thus resulting in speculation or no guess at all. There is no large data base that will provide answers to all our questions, but we do know that a serious problem exists today with nuisance wildlife.

In the chapters ahead you will get an overview of how to cope with nuisance animals and learn much more about the problems and solutions of many nuisance species. Keep in mind, though, that it is we who have started the trouble with our increasing population and exploding developments. Also, remember that all wildlife is a necessary resource for every human. Personally, I would much rather learn to coexist with problem animals than to do away with any species.

CHAPTER 3

Coping with Wildlife Problems and Damages

Throughout North America, people maintain a wide range of wildlife values. These values embrace a variety of concerns, from the preservation and protection of wildlife to the extermination of troublesome animals. Most citizens and wildlife officials believe that animal damage solutions are often necessary. Conflicts between man and animal, resulting in economic loss or threats to human health and safety, have led to major research programs to reduce human and wildlife conflicts.

In recent years, I have watched birds of prey carry helpless chickens away, coyotes stalk tame mallard ducks on a nearby farm pond located in the middle of a residential district, foxes dine out repeatedly on domesticated turkeys, and white-tailed deer totally demolish a vegetable garden. Yet these are but a few examples of the losses that have occurred as a result of nuisance animals. Other people have experienced far worse problems with animals. Most individuals, however, regardless of the type of damages they endure, look for answers to persistent conflicts.

Potential solutions to many conflicts between man and animal are vast and vary from species to species. The following chapters will provide answers to dealing with many problem animals that you may encounter, though it should be noted that circumstances may affect the outcome of the suggested solutions. After all, animal behavior is often unpredictable. One word of caution, however, should apply to all those who suffer from animal damage. Before choosing a remedy, you should understand that some methods may pose a threat to another animal species that was not the responsible party. One example could be the use of poison. While poison could provide a solution to a particular animal, it could also endanger domestic animals, plants, fish, or other wildlife species that did not relate to the problem or cause harm to humans. Your success in controlling the nuisance animal, whether it be a woodchuck in the garden, a family of raccoons that have set up permanent residence under your home, or a diseased animal that threatens your health, will depend on your ability to identify the problem and species and your skill in dealing with the damage causing animal.

For just a moment, I should say something about hunting. As we have become more suburbanized in recent decades, many people have failed to realize the importance of hunting and trapping. However, hunting and trapping are perhaps the least expensive ways to bring about a solution to nuisance animals. Wildlife officials support hunting and trapping and believe they are the most effective tools for managing wildlife populations. Without annual harvests, we would most certainly experience far more problems with some animals than we do now. I would recommend that all readers see the last chapter of this book. It will explain more about an overpopulation of animals that have become wildlife pests.

Before one can solve animal problems, they must first know where to begin. Whom do they contact and what action should they take once they have contacted the proper authorities? Surprisingly to some, a remedy may only be a phone call away. But before I provide this helpful information, it will be in your best interest to know the following: The problem animal should first be identified; you must be aware of the damage it has caused or the threat it poses. Once you have recognized these factors, you are a major step closer to getting help.

The possibility exists that you may not need outside help to resolve the problem. Victims of problem animals can discuss their situation with officials to see if the conflict is potentially hazardous or damaging. Many problems that are strictly incidental may not require a drastic solution. Also, the animal that appears to be a nuisance could be doing you favors.

You may remember in Chapter 2 my discussion about bats and how frequently urban people complain about their presence. One individual claimed that human disturbance to hibernating and maternity colonies and the all too prevalent attitude that "the only good bat is a dead bat" have been important factors in declining bat populations. According to many specialists though, bats do not get in your hair, carry rabies or suck your blood (now you know they can't turn you into a vampire). In fact, I welcome the sight of bats near my home simply because they reduce insects. It has been estimated that a single bat can eat 3,000 or more insects each night.

Making a "Positive ID" of animal pests is easier said than done, though it is vital to your success in coping with the problem. Identifying the problem animal can even be difficult for a wildlife specialist if you offer little assistance. However, your overall knowledge of wildlife will play an important role in your ability to recognize the nuisance animal. I consider myself to be quite knowledgeable when it comes to the behavior and habits of many wildlife species, simply because I have spent years studying and photographing wildlife. Yet when a predator raided my chicken house regularly (for several consecutive weeks a chicken was either killed and left to rot, killed and consumed, or disappeared off the face of the earth), I could not positively identify the animal causing the problem. I narrowed it down to an opossum, raccoon, fox, mink, weasel or domestic cat. That's quite a long list, but I found it necessary to consider every possibility before achieving a solution.

Incidentally, at the time of this writing I have not yet identified the pest, but I did stop the killing by tightening up the poultry house. Any openings that would allow a nocturnal visitor to prey on the chickens were closed, thus preventing further damage. Actually, more than one of the pests I mentioned could have been responsible for the chicken losses. It is not very unusual for one predator to sneak in and take advantage of the gold mine that another discovered. This may frequently occur when a dominating predator decides to take control. A coyote, for example, considers the fox an enemy and will not hesitate to challenge the carnivore if necessary.

To identify the nuisance critter, you should look for tracks and scat. Nothing beats visual contact with the problem animal, but seldom does this occur because many problem animals do not become active until after dark. On the other hand some nocturnal species will prey or make regular visitations to residential food sources in the daylight hours, particularly when they continue to

You must first identify the nuisance animal, sometimes without seeing it, before you can deal with the problem. For instance, you will seldom see the coyote in daylight hours, but tracks or scat near the damage area will provide proof.

get away with the same crime day after day.

I have provided several illustrations of animal tracks in this book to help you identify some species of wildlife. Every animal track is unique and should be unmistakable when the time comes to identify the species that left its mark. In addition, I have provided photographs of some animals to guide you through the identification process.

When it becomes necessary for you to obtain tracks, you may want to consider building a base to get the tracks. Sometimes you can make mud by soaking the ground with water just before dusk. When pursuing black bear in a few Northwestern states and Ontario, and finding it necessary to know how large a bear I was dealing with, I have used flour or sand to obtain tracks. You must put your base where the critter will soon be, however. An opening in a fence or building, for instance, would be an excellent location if the animal utilizes these openings.

Several quality books that focus entirely on animal behavior, identification of the species and their tracks are also available at book stores and libraries. I would strongly recommend you obtain these books if you do not find the answers in the chapters ahead.

One inexpensive book, *Peterson First Guides — Urban Wildlife*, published by Houghton Mifflin Co., provides illustrations of various species of wildlife that you may encounter. Another fine book is *Animal Tracks and Signs of North America*, published by Stackpole Books. This illustrated guidebook provides numerous photos of tracks and scat left behind by many species of wildlife.

A comprehensive reference book used by many wildlife biologists is also available to the general public. *Prevention and Control of Wildlife Damage* is fully illustrated and outlines and explains all currently registered and recommended control measures and materials. It is available from the University of Nebraska, 202 Natural Resources Hall, Lincoln, NE 68583-0819.

Once you have identified the pest, options become available. You may be permitted to dispose of the animal by live trapping and transporting it elsewhere (do not take it to your neighbor's yard), or kill it by shooting, trapping or poisoning the critter. You can also consider eliminating the source that has attracted the animal. This could include food or perhaps the animal's habitat. In some cases, deleting habitat may discourage the animal. In other situations, you can build habitat so that the animal stays away from personal property. Finally, you may consider a barrier to keep the animal out or use a repellent to discourage it from making consistent visitations.

Before deciding which method to use, I strongly urge you to notify the proper authorities. For instance, it may be unlawful to proceed with some of the previous mentioned solutions without receiving authorization from a conservation officer or another specialist of a different service. Even if the problem animal does not fall under a particular individual's jurisdiction, they can probably direct you to the proper agency.

Many animals, such as this immature bald eagle, are federally protected. First decide what agency can provide assistance before taking action.

Game and fish departments on the state and provincial levels are responsible for many species of game animals within their boundaries, such as furbearing animals and some migratory species. However, some endangered and threatened species, along with migratory birds, fall under the responsibility of the USDI's (U.S. Department of the Interior) Fish and Wildlife Service. Laws vary from state to state and province to province, so there are no certain rules that apply to all species.

ADC officials on the local level may also be of assistance, or can at least advise you as to the organization that can help. The USDA/APHIS with the cooperation of the ADC program also provides technical assistance to control problems caused by wild-life that are to complex for any one individual, group or agency to solve. Since 1985 the USDA/APHIS/ADC have worked to mini-mize the effects of wildlife on livestock and crops and to protect human health and safety from wildlife damage.

To give you an example, a Montana rancher enclosed 60 acres of land with an eight-foot-high mesh fence and four electric out-side wires to exclude predators from killing 900 pheasants. The fence proved effective and kept the coyotes and other ground preda-tors from killing his pheasants. However, eagles and hawks soon took over the dirty job of feasting on the rancher's pheasants. ADC responded by recommending habitat modifications within the en-closure and construction of an overhead wire-grid system to dis-courage the birds of prey. ADC also suggested a number of scare tactics. According to ADC officials, the number of pheasants killed by raptors significantly decreased.

ADC may also provide assistance for the following animal damage circumstances:

- crops and livestock
- natural resources
- public and private property
- bird hazards to aircraft
- starling and blackbird contamination at feedlots
- bird damage to aquaculture
- urban starling and blackbird roosts
- nuisance Canada geese
- predation of waterfowl and livestock
- beaver flooding roads and damaging timber
- deer damaging orchards, crops, and landscapes
- bear destroying timber and beehives
- wildlife-borne diseases, such as rabies and plague
- wildlife threats to endangered species

The ability to deal with nuisance animals often becomes frus-trating. This frequently leads to unnecessary harm to both wildlife and the environment if the victims do not fully understand the solutions. ADC, with its qualified wildlife biologists, though, ensures that responses to damage will be biologically sound and economically efficient.

Apparently the services provided by ADC have been widely appreciated. According to a random survey conducted by ADC during 1993, 90 percent of 1,650 direct control customers claimed they were satisfied with the level of service they received from ADC, and 96 percent stated that they believed their wildlife damage would have increased without ADC assistance.

You can also report a problem to your local Cooperative Extension Service. An agent may provide an array of information on how to prevent and control wildlife damage. You can find their listing in the U.S. government section of telephone directories.

As for receiving help from state and provincial game and fish departments, you may find they offer various noteworthy types of assistance. Many will provide habitat management tips so that you can prevent, reduce or eliminate wildlife problems in a given area. This usually involves the construction or modification of food and cover for wildlife (see Chapter 9). These officials may also provide technical assistance through advice, written materials, training and demonstrations to help you cope with nuisance animals. In some cases, they may even donate equipment to assist you with the problem species.

In New Hampshire, service is provided to citizens in three basic ways, including loaning equipment to those experiencing wildlife damage. For example, in fiscal year 1993 the state provided more than 106,502 linear feet of electric fence (included chargers and fencing configurations), 830 frightening device units, 66 traps that were in compliance with state policy and 46.5 gallons of repellents.

The 1993 survey conducted by the Minnesota Department of Natural Resources (mentioned in Chapter 2) to which 43 states responded included an assessment of agency responsibilities. In other words, there are various agencies that accept the responsibility for wildlife damage control and abatement in each state. Agencies include the following: State Wildlife Agency; State Agriculture Agency; USDA; USDI U.S. Fish and Wildlife Service; Cooperative Extension Service; County/Township/Municipal; Other (Co-op, health department and private organization).

Although many organizations may provide assistance when you seek help with nuisance animals, be aware that a particular agency may only offer a certain type of assistance for a given species. For instance, one agency may supply a necessary permit to remove a problem animal but limit these permits to certain species. Other agencies may only provide information about some species, though they may offer technical assistance with a different species.

As previously discussed, in the U.S. and Canada, federal and/ or state/province laws may also apply regarding the solution to a problem species of which you seek assistance. In Indiana where I reside, you do not need a permit to remove certain animals on your own property during a closed season, providing the animal is in the act of damaging property. The law allows owners and tenants of any property to do so if they report it to a conservation officer or the Director of the Division of Fish and Wildlife within a given number of hours. To remove some species, though, you must first obtain a permit. The laws in your state/province may differ totally, so you should contact authorities prior to taking any action.

According to officials in Nova Scotia, the owner or occupier of the property involved with nuisance wildlife must first use all reasonable methods to scare away the offending animal. This provides a defense to any charge that the individual is harassing wildlife. Secondly, a conservation officer may issue a permit to destroy the offending wildlife if scaring the animal failed.

Local authorities often provide assistance in urban areas, as do private organizations. Many times they will assist urban residents or take full control of removing the nuisance animal. Free-roaming cats and dogs require much of their attention but wild animals are no longer strangers in many urban areas due to the expansion of many cities into the country.

In case you believe that only homeowners and landowners suffer from animal damage, you are very wrong. ADC consistently manages wildlife damage problems on public lands, particularly those under the responsibility of the USDA's Forest Service and the USDI's Fish and Wildlife Service. Most land management agencies request and authorize assistance from ADC for various reasons, but predation on livestock is the most common problem. Occasionally, though, people ask ADC to remove wildlife that poses a threat to public safety on these lands.

Throughout this book I have used the term "nuisance animal." However, what constitutes a nuisance animal to one individual may not to another. For instance, a person may see a coyote walk through their yard and consider it a nuisance. Others, such as myself, see it only as a wild animal doing whatever it happens to be doing. Those who automatically become alarmed with the

Many people, upon seeing an animal such as a black bear, would express immediate fear. However, an animal sighting does not necessarily call for the removal of an animal.

sighting may also seek unnecessary assistance. Thus, removing the animal could be a waste of time and money for those who would deal with the problem. An attempt to remove the animal alive could also endanger the species unnecessarily. In a previous chapter, I discussed human fear of animal sightings. In my opinion, fear of a particular species is no reason to have it removed. Instead, learn all you can about the animal you see — remembering the old saying, "Knowledge conquers fear."

When damage occurs or an animal appears threatening to property and human health, you could consider it to be a nuisance. Many individuals even run commercial operations that deal with nuisance animals. They, too, must obey laws and operate effectively to remain in business. Depending on these laws, operators may kill, or trap and release some species of animals. Some commercial operators must also complete annual reports that show how they provided assistance to those in need.

Table 14 shows how commercial operators in Michigan during 1994 dealt with some species of nuisance animals. As you will see, with certain species there were more animals trapped and released than killed. However, this is not to say that you should not kill some nuisance animals. In many situations, killing the animal

Species	Total Complaints	Total Released	Total Killed
Bats (Non-Protected)	1,087	742	76
Beaver	368	0	877
Coyote	59	0	41
Fox	18	6	30
Muskrat	261	48	752
Opossum	1,198	1,079	467
Raccoon	5,410	5,951	1,542
Skunk	2,444	2,187	456
Squirrel	2,894	2,785	542

Table 14. The disposal method of some species of nuisance animals in Michigan during 1994. Source: Michigan Department of Natural Resources.

is the only effective solution to the problem. Simply said, many circumstances will affect the outcome of a nuisance animal problem.

According to the 1994 Illinois Nuisance Wildlife Control Summary, the department has encouraged euthanization of common game and furbearing mammals because relocation can: (1) spread diseases to resident populations, (2) compound nuisance wildlife problems in nearby residential areas, (3) increase predation of Neotropical migrants and their eggs, and (4) disrupt social and behavioral mechanisms in resident populations. The proportion of animals euthanized or taken by lethal means (58 percent) exceeded the proportion released (Table 15).

Scott Parks, an avid Indiana trapper for more than 15 years, operates commercially whenever conservation officers notify him. When Parks traps nuisance animals during the closed season (many furs are in poor condition at this time of the year and have little value), he may find it necessary to charge a fee for his services. This helps to recover many of the major expenses he encounters, such as the mileage he travels to set and run a trap line.

Species	Released	Percentage
Bat	1,480	86%
Beaver	108	6%
Coyote	5	2%
Fox	13	16%
Muskrat	165	5%
Opossum	2,418	53%
Raccoon	5,832	44%
Striped Skunk	35	1%
Squirrel	5,143	60%
Woodchuck	1,226	30%

Table 15. Total number of captured animals released and percentage of those relocated by nuisance wildlife control permittees in Illinois, 1994. Source: Illinois Department of Conservation.

Parks has specialized in trapping both raccoon and beaver. However, he has noticed a rise in nuisance animal complaints in recent years, particularly those involving these two species. He blames the drop in fur prices, fewer trappers and rising populations of many furbearing animals.

"About 15 years ago, a quality raccoon or beaver fur would bring about $25 to $35, and you could even get $6 or more for a muskrat. This made trapping more profitable. But the average price today for a raccoon or beaver is about $13 or $14, and the muskrat has dropped to about $2.50 per hide," explained Parks.

As for the price most people pay a commercial operator for their services, Parks said it varies. But he claims that some commercial trappers will charge $50 to $75 per animal. He added that many people will gladly pay this price to get rid of animals causing damage.

Trapping is truly an art, learned primarily through experience. A qualified trapper knows the habits of the animal he pursues and can apply the necessary skills to remove the animal. The trapper also finds it necessary to use a variety of types and sizes of traps.

Trapping is seldom the only answer to ridding yourself of a problem animal, however. In fact, it may be possible to prevent a problem with a nuisance animal, or discourage the animal by removing or building wildlife habitat. All too often we destroy large areas of wildlife habitat, and this leads to frequent conflicts between man and animal. I often consider dense plantings to produce habitat. I have practiced this technique and enjoyed it immensely, simply because of the wildlife viewing opportunities and the satisfaction of knowing that I have provided an animal with its necessary habitat.

Nuisance animals may also peak at certain times of the year. Seasonal influences, such as food availability or cover, are often the reason why many species of animals become a problem. For instance, in 1993 and 1994 the Missouri Department of Conservation received more complaints requiring on-site visits during May. Missouri received more complaints about black bear in May, June and July in 1993, and in May, June and August in 1994. White-tailed deer caused more problems in September during 1993, and

This deer doesn't hesitate to jump a fence to feed on an agricultural handout. Many people don't approve of their hard-earned dollars feeding a herd of deer, while others appreciate the wildlife viewing opportunity.

August in 1994. Overall, Missouri officials have determined that the major concerns occur from March through November each year.

Arkansas also reported more nuisance black bear complaints in May and July than during any other months during 1994. The state claimed that natural food supplies, localized reproductive rates and other factors can affect the total number of nuisance bear complaints in any given month or area.

No doubt, coping with nuisance animals is a complex subject because there are so many different laws governing the handling of certain species. The average individual may also find that they need to contact a particular agency that provides the help they seek. But with determination, you can resolve the problems in a safe and economical manner.

If you wish to contact a government agency or an organization mentioned in this book, refer to the Appendix.

CHAPTER 4

Birds and Waterfowl

I believe it safe to assume that everyone loves birds, regardless of their occasional bad habits or nasty behavior. Some sing magical tunes that provide peace and happiness to our souls. Others are simply a joy to see. Many species of birds, however, can become a nuisance to the homeowner, landowner, commercial poultry farmer, or pen-reared game bird operator.

The homeowner/landowner often suffers damage and losses, or experiences a health hazard as a result of too many roosting birds. Damage to lawns, gardens, crops, pets and poultry often occurs, compliments of our feathered friends.

But the damage extends far beyond the homeowner/landowner. For instance, the National Sunflower Association reported that the total direct economic impact of blackbird damage in 1994 is estimated at $73.1 million. As for the cost of control, a survey indicated that producers spent about $767,000 for prevention equipment and more than 90,000 hours attempting to control the problem.

Airports have also had their bird-related woes. Chicago's O'hare International Airport, one of the world's largest and busiest, reported 70 bird/aircraft strikes in 1992. These strikes resulted in $8 million in damage to aircraft.

According to a 1995 USDA/APHIS factsheet, the first reported wildlife/aircraft strike occurred in 1912 when a Model EX Wright Pusher collided with a gull and crashed into the ocean, killing the pilot. Since 1912, the problems have steadily worsened.

A large flock of starlings and gulls collided with a plane taking off at Boston's Logan Airport in 1960, resulting in 62 human deaths. A jet fighter struck a mallard duck on takeoff in 1988. At the John F. Kennedy International Airport in 1975, an engine of an airplane exploded and separated from the aircraft when it sucked in herring gulls. The plane caught fire and was destroyed, but fortunately no fatalities occurred because 139 passengers that happened to be airline employees were trained in evacuation procedures.

Many bird/aircraft collisions occur because our feathered friends compete for air space with the aircraft. In fact, the problems are serious enough that ADC biologists provide airport officials across the nation with advice and recommendations on how to keep runways and flight paths clear of wildlife. The Federal Aviation Administration estimate wildlife causes $35 million in damages each year to aircraft in this country. In addition, there are indirect costs such as flight delays, aircraft changes and loss of revenue.

On the positive side, though, birds are extremely valuable to man. They eat large quantities of food, including insects that can be hazardous to orchards, crops, or perhaps trees and shrubs surrounding your home. However, some have earned the title of "birds of prey.

Hawks and Owls

Birds of prey, known as raptors, include a variety of species. Falcons, eagles and ospreys are no doubt birds of prey, but it is often hawks and owls that cause major problems for man due to their daily consumption of chickens, turkeys, farm-raised ducks and geese or pen-reared game birds. Of course, few raptors come to rely on farm-raised birds as their next meal. Most birds of prey feed on other wildlife and insects. However, the birds of prey have been known to get into a bad habit once they discover an easy meal. They have even taken advantage of small dogs and cats, though it is uncommon.

It took very little research for me to learn that there are about 20 species of owls and more than a dozen species of hawks in North America. Only a few species of owls and hawks usually become a nuisance, however.

Of the various species of owls, the barn, barred and great horned owl often receive the blame for poultry and other farm-raised bird losses. These mystical, nocturnal hunters do their dirty work near dawn and dusk, or in the midnight hours, flying silently to swoop down on their unsuspecting victims.

The barn owl is found throughout most of the U.S. except for some Northwest states, and in the southern portions of some Canadian provinces. It typically has the heart-shaped "monkey face" and appears buff and brown with gray blemishes on its feathers. It can reach a height of about 18 inches and prefers to live near woodland edges, in marshes or, you guessed it, barns. This shy creature loves abandoned homesteads nestled in rural areas. It feeds on rodents and insects, but will occasionally feed on poultry.

"Who cooks for you, who cooks for you all?" That is the common sounds of the barred owl found from the farthest eastern point in southern Canada, south to the Gulf of Mexico. The barred owl can grow larger than the barn owl and is known for its rounded head and dark streaks on the belly. It lives in the woods of dense forests, farm country and marshes, and eats mice, small animals and birds.

The great horned owl, widely distributed throughout most of North America, is responsible for most nuisance complaints involving owls. They do not hesitate to prey on larger animals

Birds of prey, such as this barred owl, are nocturnal but may do their hunting near dawn and dusk. They can fly very quietly and surprise poultry without warning.

such as rabbits or even full-grown chickens. They have also been known to kill other owls, Canada geese and swans. They commonly feed at night but may not hesitate to feed on livestock during the daylight hours if they do not feel threatened. Considering their size, it's no wonder that this bird of prey hopes to get a mouthful when the hunting begins.

A full-grown great horned owl can reach a height of 30 inches or more. The large ear tuffs are responsible for its name, though it does not have horns. However, some people do claim that it has potent ears. Habitats include a variety of terrain, from open ranges to dense woods. They have also set up temporary homes in urban districts.

When poultry or other farm-reared bird losses occur, it can be difficult to determine whether or not a bird of prey was responsible. Many furbearing animals also feed on poultry. However, raptors seldom kill more than one chicken or turkey per day. Each animal that does feed on poultry, though, seems to have a distinctive killing habit. The owl often tears the head and neck away, and will sometimes pluck the feathers from its victim. It may also swallow its food whole. Furbearing animals usually tear into their victims, often leaving behind messy evidence.

Of the forest hawks, the northern goshawk causes most hawk-related livestock losses. Of the soaring hawks, the red-tailed usually receives the blame.

The goshawk feeds on forest rodents but may be attracted to poultry if it becomes available within its range (Alaska to New Mexico). It feeds on animals as large as rabbits but prefers large birds. Its close cousin, the cooper's hawk, is smaller than the adult 20-inch goshawk.

The ear-piercing sound of the red-tailed hawk, common when the bird sees man and furbearing predators, is the most widely distributed hawk in North America. It soars and hunts throughout all of the U.S. and most of Canada. Various color phases exist but most are identifiable by their dark brown or reddish brown tail feathers.

Although red-tailed hawks prey on rodents and mice consistently (sometimes at the site of kill), I have also watched them carry off rabbits. On one occasion I heard the cries of a cottontail rabbit in distress. Almost as quickly, I found myself looking upwards to see a red-tailed hawk more than 60 feet in the air carrying a rabbit.

Shortly before this chapter started, my writing was interrupted by the shrill screams of chickens. This sound of alarm I have heard many times before, so I wasted little time in heading for the chicken pen to determine the problem. When I walked out the backdoor, I heard the "peep-peep-peep" of a chick. A red-tailed hawk then went airborne with the two-week-old chick clutched in its claws.

Red-tailed hawks are somewhat territorial and will not hesitate to stay in one good hunting area. In fact, the hawk that took the chick stuck around for several days. I assumed he was the same one, simply because I saw him daily for a week. He did not get any more chicks because there were no more to be gotten. However, he did attempt to retrieve an adult hen, changing his mind only when I came to the chicken's rescue. The hen was stripped of her back feathers when the raptor attempted to latch onto her, but was unharmed.

When hawks feed on poultry at the location of their attack, they almost always pluck their victim's feathers. If a portion of the carcass remains, you may also see punctures caused by the hawk's beak.

Hawks and owls are federally protected in the U.S. and Canada and cannot be captured or killed without a permit. However, it is not unlawful to scare, or attempt to scare the bird of prey. For more information contact your local conservation officer, USDA/ APHIS/ADC agent, or the U.S. Fish and Wildlife Service.

Guns, particularly shotguns, may be effective in frightening a hawk or owl but should not be aimed at a bird of prey. Firecrackers may also work to scare away the raptor. Before using a shotgun or firecracker, though, check to see if the law permits them in the area where the problem occurs.

It may be easier to accept poultry losses caused by hawks or owls if you remember that they do far more good than harm. They eat their share of undesirable rodents such as mice and rats as well as some of the ugliest insects you have ever seen.

Preventing attacks on poultry, pigeons and farm-reared fowl or game birds is the wisest choice. I do not suffer losses in the dark hours because I have made it a point to close off any openings in the chicken house that would allow a predator to enter while the chickens roost. One could go a step further by using a fence to confine the animals and netting to protect them from above, or simply by keeping them in a dwelling. Finally, if the farm-raised birds are kept outside in the daylight hours, allow the surrounding vegetation to grow thick, thus providing cover so that birds of prey do not easily spot them from above. The dense vegetation will also serve as an escape avenue for the farm-raised birds.

Gulls and Herons

Several species of birds enjoy eating fish. Cormorants, herons, egrets, gulls and pelicans often include fish in their daily menu, along with a variety of other foods. However, herons are the real bad apples when it comes to a fishy meal.

Four species of herons roam North America, but the great blue heron is the most common. This prehistoric looking bird may reach a height of four feet or more and has a wingspread up to seven feet. It prefers to spend most of its time near ponds, lakes, marshes and rivers. The great blue heron builds large nests using sticks in trees.

Homeowners/landowners with lakes and ponds that have large quantities of fish may suffer occasional fish losses from herons and other fish-eating birds. But for various reasons they may never know that the fish-eating birds have visited a waterhole. Obvious signs are herons roosting in trees near the water, herons seen standing in or near the water, nests and tracks of fish-eating birds. It is also possible that you may find partially eaten fish, though most herons swallow the fish whole. The great blue heron, primarily a daytime feeder, will eat fish ranging from minnows to those several inches long.

This great blue heron feeds on a mouse. Others will not hesitate to feed on fish at hatcheries, or perhaps in your pond.

Fish farmers often suffer great losses, particularly in the Eastern U.S., where millions of dollars worth of various species of fish are grown and harvested annually. According to a USDA/APHIS/ADC report, American aquaculturists raise about 900 million pounds of fish each year, with some operations reporting annual losses caused by fish-eating birds in excess of $200,000. Fish-eating birds also prey on endangered and rare species of fish.

ADC encourages the use of netting, wire grids, and fencing because these devices offer fish farmers long-term protection. However, the cost often makes physical barriers impractical. ADC also recommends frightening techniques — noise-making devices, such as propane cannons and cracker shells. Visual tools, like helium balloons, remote-control boats and airplanes, large pieces of foil and scarecrows may also be effective. However, noise-making devices and visual tools tend to provide only temporary relief. The fish-eating birds quickly adapt to the sight and sound of the frightening devices.

Landfills located near an impoundment or fish farm will usually attract many fish-eating birds, but particularly gulls. Gulls enjoy scavenging on almost anything digestible (and some indigestible items), but do not mind leaving the dump and traveling a short distance to find fresh fish. Guard dogs may help to deter these fish-eating birds from making regular visitations (local leash laws may apply).

On one occasion, gulls caused roof damage and paint damage to automobiles at an automobile manufacturing facility in Chesterfield, Michigan. ADC officials successfully relocated the 2,000-bird colony by removing nests and eggs and by frightening the birds with noise-making devices and other scare tactics.

A hatchery manager in Washington estimated fish-eating birds killed approximately $50,000 worth of salmon and steelhead fingerling fish. Gulls and great blue herons accounted for much of the loss. ADC specialists constructed an overhead wire-grid exclusion system over the ponds that significantly reduced the fish losses.

Individuals who experience losses caused by fish-eating birds will need to try a frightening technique since the birds are federally protected and classified as migratory. Permits may be granted to take lethal action (trapping or killing), but only after frightening techniques have been tried. The homeowner/landowner could try firecrackers or shotgun blasts, or, if lawful, alarm and automatic exploding devices. In addition, it may also be beneficial to remove roost sites near the impoundment. Keep in mind, though, many fish-eating birds do little damage to impoundments and instead offer enjoyable viewing opportunities. For more assistance contact a USDA wildlife damage control biologist in your region.

Ducks and Geese

There are hundreds of species of ducks and geese in North America, most of which migrate. Most migrate to survive, finding their way to food and water, though some will come to depend upon a given area and move very little. These waterfowl often become nuisances for various reasons.

Waterfowl are valuable natural resources as far as the general public is concerned. But nonmigrating ducks and geese have increased throughout North America, often selecting one area for swimming, resting, breeding and raising young. These areas include residential districts, commercial property and public areas where people consistently spend time.

Ducks and geese that inhabit these areas often become tame and create a multitude of problems, from the overgrazing of grass and shrubs to accumulations of droppings and feathers. Aggressive birds have also attacked humans. In addition, an abundance of nuisance waterfowl has contaminated reservoirs, beaches, docks and golf courses. Farmers may also suffer major losses of crops, including corn, rice and soybeans.

I know of one family that lives in the suburbs only a couple of miles from a small town. However, several small ponds are located within a few hundred yards of the community where they reside. Mallard ducks moved into the impoundments a few years ago and set up permanent residence. The family I speak of enjoys fishing in their pond but often finds it difficult to cast their lures because the mallards get in their way. Today, it is even difficult to drive through the area because ducks are always standing in the middle of the road.

About 50 Canada geese once caused a health risk at a school for the mentally handicapped in Virginia. Numerous golf courses have also induced many flocks of geese to set up permanent residence. Players often find themselves delayed because they must move the geese. Even worse, they find themselves ankle-deep in droppings.

The best way to control waterfowl is to avoid sending an invitation. Individuals in residential and business districts should never feed waterfowl (it is not uncommon to find food morsels in areas where geese have become a nuisance). Once these birds receive handouts, they often stay. Waterfowl are quite capable of feeding on their own, but they appreciate grazing opportunities such as short, green grass. Allowing grass to grow taller will also discourage ducks and geese.

ADC officials also recommend planting vegetation other than grass along water edges. Pachysandra, periwinkle and euonymus are usually less attractive to the birds. Fences, hedgerows or other physical barriers will discourage waterfowl because they prefer to land on water and walk onto connecting grassy areas to feed and rest.

You should not construct islands or peninsulas in impoundments since waterfowl prefer to build their nests on these protected, undisturbed grounds. You can control local populations of waterfowl if property owners stop the ducks and geese from nesting.

Most pairs of geese begin breeding in late February and early March. The goslings may be born as soon as early May in many areas. However, since the goslings cannot fly for the next two months, the adults are sure to stick around and may become pests.

Removing waterfowl, or their eggs and nests, is an effective way to stop nesting but the U.S. Fish and Wildlife Service or state wildlife management agencies must first issue a permit. Waterfowl are protected by state and federal laws in the U.S. and Canada except for some species during the hunting seasons. Before receiving a permit, the applicant must prove that nonlethal habitat-management techniques were unsuccessful in controlling the problem.

You may also consider using dogs to keep ducks and geese away, though local leash laws may apply. Most species of wildlife quickly adjust to a penned or leashed dog and will not hesitate to stay beyond the dog's reach. A free-roaming dog, if trained to chase birds, will discourage waterfowl from landing. Still, I have a real problem with free-roaming dogs, simply because of other species of wildlife that may be affected by their presence (see more on dogs in Chapter 5).

Predators will certainly influence waterfowl to leave a preferred area. Mallard ducks that settled into a pond behind my home attempted to raise young on two occasions. However, predators consistently feasted on the ducklings, finally forcing the hen and drake to move elsewhere to raise a family.

Geese are often trapped and transported by state/provincial

Although waterfowl are valuable resources, nonmigrating ducks and geese have caused many problems for residential and commercial districts.

wildlife officials when severe problems occur. For example, if more than 100 birds create a problem in residential districts in Indiana, the state may provide help if a petition is signed by at least 51 percent of the surrounding property owners.

Farmers who suffer losses caused by waterfowl have a few options to alleviate the problem. First, lure crops can be planted in selected areas where damage occurs. Second, they can consider baiting by placing desired grains in preferred areas. However, it is recommended that you don't be stingy. If the bait runs dry before the ducks and geese are satisfied, they may cause additional damage when they move on and feed elsewhere. Finally, crop growers can hunt waterfowl or allow others to do so during the hunting seasons, where safe. Hunting will reduce populations and repel waterfowl. First, check your state/provincial regulations for season dates and harvest quotas.

As is the case with other nuisance birds, you can also use noise and visual devices to discourage waterfowl. You might consider a mild form of harassment, such as clapping hands or banging aluminum pans together. Shotguns (fired away from waterfowl), and automatic exploders may frighten the birds, as do helium balloons, flags, flashing lights and scarecrows.

Many lawn and garden stores, as well as mail-order catalogs, sell noise and visual devices you may want to try. Some noise makers begin when they detect body heat or motion. There are electric and battery-operated devices that you can consider, but those noise devices that are automatic and emit alarm sounds at regular intervals may provide the best results. I should mention something about visual and noise devices, however. Many people claim that they are only a temporary solution if left standing in one location. When using such devices, consider moving them daily.

CHAPTER 5

Carnivorous Animals

Carnivorous animals are those that eat flesh. Most carnivores are also predators. A predatory animal stalks and preys upon other animals. However, some carnivores also eat food other than meat. They are known as omnivores. The diet of these omnivores varies. Some may eat meat occasionally, but dine on lush vegetation, berries and other foliage. For instance, the coyote may rely on his predatory abilities and eat flesh most of the time. Bears, on the other hand, seldom feed on meat if other foods are abundant.

I have found, though, that most carnivores are intelligent and great hunters. Some are masters of locating prey and some of stalking prey. Some have good eyesight, while others have a better sense of smell. Seemingly, if a carnivorous animal lacks ability in one of its senses, Mother Nature makes up for it in another.

Because of their ability to kill, many people consider carnivorous animals to be a major nuisance. Some carnivores may attack pets, livestock and occasionally even humans. In recent years, some carnivores have even found it easier to prey upon livestock than to hunt wild animals. Although several factors cause this, it usually happens when there are fewer wild animals to prey upon and/or too many predators in a given area. Man's expansion into the carnivore's territory, an abundance of livestock and fewer trappers have resulted in some carnivorous animals becoming nuisances.

Black Bear

Although the black bear is a timid, mysterious animal that prefers solitude, it has caused more problems than any other species of bear. This is only logical, since the grizzly, brown and polar bears inhabit fewer areas than the black bear.

The black bear has adapted well to man's intrusion and continues to thrive in almost all of Canada and the U.S. In fact, they are found within the boundaries of most states. Only a few in the Midwest and South no longer have black bears.

Despite protests from some animal activists that black bear populations are dwindling, their numbers have actually increased significantly in many areas. The provinces of Canada are home to about 400,000 black bears. Alaska has about 60,000, with many other states claiming to have 20,000 or more black bears.

Black bears can survive in a variety of habitats, from the Rocky Mountains to the deciduous forests. They also inhabit the swamps and farmlands of some regions, many times within a few miles of large cities.

Several color variations of black bear exist, though some are more prominent in given areas. Of the bears I saw in Idaho from 1993 to 1996, for example, at least half were not black. I saw blond, chocolate and cinnamon, while the hides of others were multicolored. Although these color variations are typical of the Rocky Mountain states, most bears in the Northeastern states are black.

The black bear is not a true hibernator. However, they may spend several of the fall and winter months in a den. While in this comatose state, they give birth. The adult sows (2.5-years-old or older) commonly have one or two cubs. One Tennessee sow I saw had three cubs by her side.

Black bears tend to look for seasonal foods, but they eat almost anything. Acorns, blueberries, huckleberries, cherries, bugs, honey, nuts and occasional small creatures and carrion will satisfy their diet. However, when these foods are unavailable, the black bear may travel into the suburbs and towns looking for whatever edible foods it can find, usually by smell. The black bear's eyesight is less than perfect, but their sense of smell is second to none.

The black bear can wreak havoc on both livestock and agricultural crops. A farmer in Pennsylvania once showed me a corn field that black bears had devastated. In fact, in one year ADC responded to more than 1,200 black bear complaints in Wisconsin alone. Most of the complaints involved bears damaging corn.

A report from the National Agricultural Statistics Service showed that bears were responsible for an estimated loss of 12,250 sheep/lambs in the U.S. in 1994. These losses amounted to more than $640,000. Another report showed bears killed 1,800 cattle in 1995 that amounted to $813,000 in damages. Black bears were the primary culprit.

Black bears are responsible for a variety of other problems equal to or surpassing the damages they cause to livestock and crops. A 1989 study found that there was an average of 556 bear complaints investigated each year in Minnesota (Table 16). In some years, DNR officials devoted more than 5,000 hours to handle bear complaints. However, officials note that harvest by hunters is the primary tool used to manage bear populations in the state.

Many people will consider

Type of Complaint	Percentage
Garbage Disturbance	43%
Threat to Humans	42%
Property Damage	26%
Crop Damage	14%
Livestock Threat/Loss	9%
Campground Nuisance	9%
Damage to Beehives	7%

Table 16. Complaints and percentage of total types of complaints received by DNR staff in Minnesota, 1981 to 1988 (totals do not add to 100% because some complaints included multiple reasons. Source: Minnesota Dept. of Natural Resources.

the black bear a nuisance upon seeing the animal. You can justify this in some cases. One New Jersey biologist told me that he received several unusual complaints about black bears during his work period with the game and fish department. He recalled one bear that he trapped and relocated. It seems the bruin had made a habit of coming to a woman's backyard pool and cooling off by taking a swim on hot summer days.

Bears also cause property damage. They often damage or destroy dumpsters, garbage cans, fences, buildings, screen porches, tents and pop-up campers as they search for food. Hunger may encourage any black bear to visit a neighborhood or campground. This frequently occurs in areas where people feed bears. These bears may also lose fear of man and begin associating humans with food.

Normally, males tend to cause more problems than do sows. One study prepared by Arkansas in 1994 showed that 96 percent of the nuisance bears handled by state officials were males. This is

An Ontario black bear visited this dump site near Gogama for three consecutive evenings. Once a bear is accustomed to a handout, it will not hesitate to return.

not uncommon, however, since many complaints are received in the summer months when boars are breeding and traveling widely in search of females. The younger boars are pushed out of some areas and forced to find new ones, which may put them close to people. But sows with cubs can create problems. This could be due to their desire to satisfy nutritional requirements, according to the Arkansas report.

Arkansas also showed "fear" and "having one near the house" as the first and second most important reasons why the state received complaints about black bears. Livestock problems were third, with garbage, crop, beehive and tree damage also reported.

Most people express fear of the black bear, and for good reason. They are powerful animals with grinding teeth and sharp claws. They can run in excess of 30 miles per hour for short distances. I have spent about 20 years hunting and photographing black bears and have come to respect them. I also use common sense when I have a close encounter. Although I have not experienced any major problems, I have been charged twice while photographing bears in the Great Smoky Mountains National Park. Both bears, however, used a bluff tactic.

Park bears are often much more dangerous than other bears in the wild because they frequently meet people. However, people cause many of the bear/human problems that occur today. I remember seeing one person try to put his daughter on a log next to a black bear. He simply wanted to get a "cute" photo. Before I could offer a warning, the bear took a clean swipe at the girl, missing her only by inches with his claws. I could not believe this even after I saw it, but have heard other similar tales. Unfortunately, officials eventually have to destroy some black bears because many individuals have no understanding of this magnificent animal.

Though black bear attacks on humans are uncommon, people provoke many of the attacks that do occur. Here are the details of a few incidents that occurred in California from 1986 to 1996: You can form your own opinions.

Park visitors are often fascinated with bears. However, this often leads to problems for both the tourist and the bear.

- In September 1986, a long-time male resident of a small rural community was injured while feeding a bear at his residence. He had been feeding bears at this location for more than 30 years.
- In May 1986, a 35-year-old man was attacked while camping in a tent. The bear left when the victim hit him with a tent pole. The man sustained several puncture wounds to his shoulder and lacerations to the back of his head.
- In August 1991, an archer hunting for deer spotted a black bear and began photographing her until he noticed that she had cubs. The bear charged, caught him and bit him repeatedly around the shoulders.

- In August 1993, two separate incidents occurred within three days. In both cases, a bear or bears grabbed a victim by the head and attempted to drag a child away while they slept on the ground in sleeping bags. The bear also inflicted minor injuries on three other campers immediately prior to the attacks. Both garbage and natural foods were available nearby.
- In April 1995, three adults received minor injuries from a young bear after capturing it, placing it in their car and driving to town because they claimed they needed to "save" the bear. Officials eventually killed the bear and tested it for rabies.

A high population of black bears is found in popular Yosemite National Park in California. Although natural foods are abundant, studies have shown that human foods comprise at least 15 percent of the bear's diet in Yosemite.

Though human injuries from black bear attacks at Yosemite have declined in recent years, the total number of incidents has remained high. Property damage as a result of black bears has also increased at Yosemite. According to a report, the state has adapted a "proactive" and "reactive" management program at preventing human/bear conflicts. The proactive management is aimed at preventing human/bear conflicts and mitigating them by providing long-term solutions. The reactive management responds to ongoing conflicts and attempts to mitigate them through immediate action (this may include capture and removal of problem bears). The plan hopes to restore and maintain the natural integrity, distribution, abundance and behavior of the indigenous black bear population. It provides for the safety of park visitors by planning the development and use of the park to prevent conflicts and unpleasant or dangerous incidents with bears.

According to a press release I received from Safari Club International at the time of this writing, a bear mauled two young girls on an Arizona mountain range. Both girls were recovering, but only after one had undergone twelve hours of surgery. The mountain range is a popular weekend getaway for area residents.

"The Arizona Game and Fish Department has already relocated five bears this summer and killed two in an effort to protect the public," said Robert Easterbrook Sr., president of Safari Club International. "At least one citation was issued to a woman who was allegedly feeding and watering the area's bears. Wildlife professionals theorize many other people have been doing the same thing, inadvertently removing their (bear's) natural fear of humans, leading to tragedies where innocent children are dragged from their campsite and mauled."

Easterbrook explained that wildlife management issues, such as those faced by a number of states, should not be decided at a ballot box. In recent years, many individuals have had the opportunity to vote on whether or not certain management practices, such as hunting black bear, should be allowed. I must agree with Easterbrook. It is our wildlife professionals that should decide this, not the public. Easterbrook also noted that the bears could be managing us, as is happening near Tucson where officials closed three campgrounds in an effort to protect the public.

Except when hunger becomes an issue, black bears are as a rule nocturnal. Damage to property and/or livestock may allow you to identify the problem animal as a black bear, as will scat and tracks. When black bears kill large animals they often crush bones. As for tracks, the hind foot is larger than the front and resembles that of man. The front foot is more rounded but claw marks usually are not visible except in mud, sand or snow.

To prevent a black bear from visiting your neighborhood, you must eliminate odors and foods, such as garbage, pet foods, fruit, compost, bird seed and barbecue grills. You can count on a bear returning once he discovers these attractants. However, if you eliminate the attractant immediately, the bear will soon become discouraged and leave.

When hiking in bear country, consider traveling with others and do not be afraid to talk. Voices and other noises will discourage most wild bears. You may also consider noisemakers, such as a can with rocks that you can tie to your clothing and equipment. When walking with the wind in your face, be alert since a bear

The front foot of a mature black bear may have a diameter of 4 to 5 inches.

ahead of you may not smell you coming.

Campers should store foods in a vehicle whenever possible. Those packing in should put foods in a bear-proof container and hang it at least twelve feet above the ground. Black bears are good tree climbers so be sure to have your food attached to a limb and well away from the trunk of the tree.

If you see a bear, always make it a point to give him space and do not run away since this could attract the bruin. The bear, if it sees you, will probably retreat. For the most part, it is a shy animal.

If you live in a black bear area, always slam doors or make other noises when coming out of the house in the dark. It is often possible to frighten a bear by clapping or shouting. When problems arise, always contact your local game and fish department. They are trained to handle situations such as this and can provide instructions for you.

Electric fences can deter black bears. Bee hive owners often use electric fences to keep bears away. Other scare tactics, such as shotguns and firecrackers also can be effective but they may provide only temporary relief. Capsaicin and red pepper spray repellent will keep bears away but are limited in effective range to about 25 feet. Ammonia placed around the visiting area of the bear may also discourage them.

Killing a bear could be illegal. Bears are protected in some states/provinces and in others can be killed only during hunting seasons with the necessary licenses/tags. Some areas do permit a landowner to dispose of the bear if it is killing livestock. As for the general public, you should not kill a bear unless it poses an immediate threat to human life or safety. In fact, individuals are often prosecuted for killing bears because they only had a fear that a bear could cause a problem.

Wildlife officials often trap and/or tranquilize problem bears, and baits are frequently used to entice the bear. After baiting bears for many years, I have found that bacon grease is an excellent attractant. I have also used anise oil and vanilla flavoring to attract bears. Trimmings of meat, fat and bones, and donuts may also keep a bear coming to the bait consistently. Most problem bears are trapped with cage-type traps, leg snares or culvert traps.

Officials usually relocate trapped bears several miles from the problem area. Though this solves the immediate problem, it does not always provide a permanent solution. A wildlife official in Ontario explained that his staff had trapped and moved 10 bears from a garbage dump and released them 70 miles away. Within one month, six of the tagged bears had returned to the dump.

Bobcats

A member of the cat family, the bobcat is recognized by its black spots, tufted ears and stubby tail. Sizes of mature bobcats vary, but most males will weigh between 15 and 30 pounds. All bobcats have a reddish-brown coat.

The bobcat's range includes the southern boundaries of the Canadian provinces, the contiguous states and Mexico. In most states their boundaries are limited to desirable habitats. For instance, we have had only a handful of bobcat sightings in Indiana during the last decade, primarily in the southern, most heavily forested portion of the state. Farming has destroyed much of the bobcat's range in many regions.

The bobcat is primarily carnivorous, feeding mostly on mice and moles. They occasionally eat rabbits and squirrels, and have been known to kill and eat wild turkeys or even deer weakened from starvation. It is an excellent hunter with superb eyesight, but this solitary predator prefers to spend its time in remote forested and rugged areas.

The tracks of a bobcat are more oval-shaped than those of a large domestic cat (Figure 5-1). They rarely exceed three inches in width and two and a half inches in length (smaller than the lynx), and because their claws are retractable you will not see claw marks. A walking bobcat will leave tracks about eight to 10 inches apart. It is not built for long runs and prefers to use its soft padded feet to stalk its prey.

Bobcats will not hesitate to feed on livestock and poultry, particularly at night if the farm-raised animals are away from the presence of man. When they kill larger animals, you may see claw marks on the back of the animal near the shoulders. Like most felines, bobcats often stalk and grab their prey. Seldom do they bite into the neck or head, as do some predators, to kill prey. It is also not unusual for them to open the animal on the underneath side along the ribs. Poultry killed by bobcats are not

Figure 5-1. Bobcat tracks seldom exceed 3 inches in width and more than 2 1/2 inches long. Illus. by Larry Smail.

easily identified because they may consume the fowl shortly after the kill. Buried or partially buried scat is a good indication that a feline created the crime. Foxes and coyotes do not bury their scat. The bobcat may also bury the remaining portion of the carcass that they have not eaten, returning later to feed.

Bobcats may kill pets occasionally. My son-in-law was forced to shoot a bobcat after it attacked his beagle hound while they hunted rabbits in eastern Kentucky. The bobcat probably felt threatened and tore into the dog's face to protect itself. The dog, incidentally, survived the attack.

Some states protect the bobcat while others consider it a game animal. Some states also consider the bobcat a legal target any time when it has killed livestock or poultry. Permits may be required, so contact your game and fish department before taking lethal action.

Like domestic/feral cats, the bobcat is an excellent climber and may get over fences. They can also jump several feet. For this reason, always use an overhead fence to keep a bobcat away from poultry.

Trapping may be effective but lures seldom attract the bobcat since it does not rely on its sense of smell as much as it does the eyes. Most traps used for foxes and coyotes will also work for bobcats. They are often lured to No. 3 or 4 leghold traps with the "fresh" remains of other animals such as chickens, rabbits and squirrels. Fur trappers often seek trapping opportunities during the fall and winter months when the bobcat's pelt is in prime condition.

Cats/Dogs

Cats and dogs, domestic or feral, cause a multitude of problems for homeowners, landowners, and our wildlife. Actually, a feral cat/dog may never have been domesticated, instead having roamed freely in a wild state from birth. Surprisingly, though, many people do not mind allowing their domestic pets to come and go as they please. They obviously have no idea how damaging their pets can be to livestock, poultry and wildlife.

Leash laws apply in some areas but many people ignore such regulations. I have also heard some say that they thought it best to take cats and dogs to the countryside and turn them loose when they could not care for them. Many people feel this is justice to the animal. But in reality, this can promptly turn a domestic pet into a starving animal that becomes the victim of a predator. The pet can also become a wild, raging killer of wildlife. Some allow their cats to come and go so that they will kill mice. Unfortunately, though, our treasured felines will kill many other animals.

A study by Dr. Stanley Temple and John Coleman of the University of Wisconsin showed that 35 percent of the rural cat's annual diet is songbirds. They also noted that many people believe a cat that wears a collar bell will alert birds to danger, but research shows cats sit and wait for their prey or stalk them very slowly. There is no time for the bird to escape by the time it hears the bell. They also claim that declawing a cat will not stop it from killing wildlife.

When cats eat a variety of birds and animals in a given area, they actually take away what another predator may have eaten. This action can promptly throw the feeding habits of other predators off balance. In addition, free-roaming cats may become hosts to several diseases.

Domestic/feral cat tracks are like those of other cats in that the claw marks cannot be identified (Figure 5-2). The tracks of large domestic cats are rounded and seldom have a diameter of more than one and a half inches.

A report from the National Agricultural Statistics Service showed that dogs killed 40,325 sheep/lambs in the U.S. in 1994. The Service also claimed that dogs killed approximately 21,800 head of cattle in the U.S. in 1995.

On many occasions I have seen dogs running white-tailed deer. When this involves a pack of dogs, the sight is not pretty. Dogs can run down a deer and kill it under certain conditions. Dogs

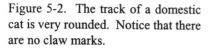

Figure 5-2. The track of a domestic cat is very rounded. Notice that there are no claw marks.

Figure 5-3. Track sizes of dogs vary, from those that compare to a coyote (up to 2 inches), and larger.

also kill fawns. I should add, many of these dogs are those that people allow to run freely.

The tracks of a domestic/feral dog can be confused with the tracks of a coyote. Although both are oval, the claw marks of the dog track are usually found closer to the toes (Figure 5-3). Track sizes of dogs also vary, whereas coyote tracks seldom exceed two inches.

When cats and dogs kill, they seldom go for the throats as many other predators do. Their victims are often mangled. In fact, dogs may attack larger animals, such as deer and livestock, from the rear first. Poultry killed by dogs is usually scattered about the attack area. Cats occasionally bite the head and the neck of poultry, but also enjoy playing with their victim by slapping and biting it before the kill.

Some states/provinces allow you to kill stray cats and dogs if they cause damage or threaten human health and safety. If the cat or dog is collared and tagged, you may be able to contact the owner or your damage control agency for further assistance. Free-roaming cats and dogs should not be handled directly since they could attack you or carry disease. You may also consider contacting an agency that deals with stray cats and dogs. However, before taking lethal action, check with local authorities.

Fencing may keep cats and dogs away from poultry and live-stock. However, cats can climb and dogs can jump or dig, so apply practical methods to discourage them. You should also eliminate any openings under the fence since dogs tend to go under fences more frequently than do foxes and coyotes. Cats may also live in buildings or under houses if you do not close off openings. You will also discourage cats and dogs by keeping garbage cans and bird feeders secured, and by not throwing food out to wild animals.

Live box traps are effective for removing undesirable cats and small dogs. For large dogs, it may be necessary to use a cage trap, leghold trap or snare. A wildlife agency can probably put you into contact with a seasoned trapper who can remove a problem cat or dog.

The worst news about free-roaming cats and dogs is their ability to live long lives and produce large litters of youngsters. A few cats and dogs in a given area can promptly turn into hundreds of problem animals in a short time.

Coyotes

At one time, the coyote inhabited only the western plains. During the last three decades, however, this canine has spread to the eastern boundaries of the U.S. and throughout most of Canada. Although some were introduced, most coyotes spread into many new areas in the early 1970s. Man has now come to realize that the coyote has not only earned the title of "prairie wolf" but also "brush wolf."

I would speculate that the coyote has expanded into many regions because it can eat a wide variety of foods. It is usually a nocturnal feeder and prefers mice and other small animals. However, its omnivorous instincts also take over occasionally. The coyote will not turn down berries, fruits and some vegetables. It has also been caught in the melon patch. Livestock and poultry losses due to coyotes have become a major problem today. But coyotes seldom raid nests and eggs as do some predators. Instead, they prefer to eat the animal that builds the nest and lays the eggs.

I would assume that you could see a coyote today in almost any given region. In fact, some people probably see coyotes and fail to recognize them as such. The coyote's long slender body is often mistaken for a dog when seen from a distance. However, one distinguishing factor is the pointed ears of the coyote. The hide can vary in color, from tan to various shades of gray. The canine's hide changes with the seasons, from thick and plush in the winter to thin and straggly in the summer.

When it comes to a mate, many wildlife specialists claim the coyote mates for life. Breeding usually occurs from December through February. A litter consists of six or more pups and can arrive as early as March. The coyote is somewhat territorial, preferring to spend most of its life within a 10-mile radius.

Coyotes have few enemies other than man. Many ranchers have set out to destroy this canine without pity. Coyotes are masters of killing sheep and have been known to do this only for sport, though most kill for food. A Colorado ranch I visited several years ago provided examples of how they kill for sport. In one small meadow, probably no larger than five acres, we found four sheep/ lambs lying dead with their throats ripped. Coyotes had not eaten any of the sheep. The rancher explained to me that the coyotes often killed to teach their pups to care for themselves.

If you read Chapter 2, you have a pretty good understanding of the coyote's role as a nuisance animal in North America. In one sentence I can refresh your memory; in 1994 the coyote killed more sheep (243,800) than any other predator; in 1995 the coyote killed about 69,350 head of cattle. But the coyote is not limited to livestock killing.

Officials at Tinker Air Force Base in Oklahoma requested assistance in 1994 from ADC when coyotes chewed through six fiber-optic lines (used in maintenance of the B-1 bomber) and damaged them beyond repair. ADC specialists resolved the problem by capturing two coyotes.

Coyotes have excellent senses but its sense of smell is probably the best. Once it smells a victim, it stalks the animal patiently or waits in ambush for the right moment to attack. Though a rabbit-sized meal will satisfy the coyote, it will not hesitate to kill a deer or antelope, particularly fawns of these species during the early summer. Coyotes also work in groups when they have a strong desire to kill a large animal.

As Figure 5-4 indicates, the tracks of a coyote appear oval and not nearly as rounded as that of a dog. They are usually about two to two and a half inches long, spaced about 12 inches apart when the coyote walks. The coyote's track is larger than that of a fox, but considerably smaller than the track of a wolf. In mud or

Figure 5-4. The track of a coyote. Notice the claw marks, common of a canine with non-retractable claws. Illus. by Larry Smail.

snow the adult coyote, which may weigh up to 30 pounds, will leave behind distinct tracks. Coyote scat often appears twisted and contains hair.

When coyotes take down livestock, such as sheep, they commonly bite the throat. Tooth marks may be present on various parts of the victim's body but the coyote usually rips open the chest cavity to feed on the heart and lungs first. Since death may come slowly, you will often see the ground torn up due to the victim thrashing.

Wolves usually live in packs. They may also kill livestock and are sometimes blamed for cattle and sheep losses, even though a coyote may be responsible. But there are differences which you may see at the site of the kill. Wolves kill in much the same manner as coyotes but may consume a small animal at one feeding. A close inspection of the victim's throat may also provide evidence that will help you determine which animal did the killing. The canine tooth of a wolf should leave a hole about one-fourth inch in diameter while the canine tooth of the coyote will leave a smaller hole (one-eighth inch or less). You should also find numerous tooth holes in the throat area if a coyote was responsible for the attack. If a wolf killed the animal you may see only one pair of holes.

When poultry losses occur frequently, the coyote often receives

When coyotes attack large animals, they usually kill by biting the throat. However, they may also feed on their victim before it is dead.

Like the coyote, the gray wolf is both a scavenger and a killer of livestock. A close examination of their prey may allow you to determine which animal is to blame.

the blame even though one or more other predators may have been responsible. A coyote will usually consume a chicken or turkey immediately following the kill, leaving little evidence other than scattered feathers. I have also seen a difference in turkeys killed by coyotes and those by foxes. The carcass that remains following when a turkey is killed by a coyote is usually not as widely scattered as one killed by a fox.

According to many officials, electric fences have done a good job of protecting livestock and poultry from coyotes. "Almost all of our producers who have constructed proper electric fences are satisfied with the results," said Eric Hutchings, regional supervisor of problem wildlife, Alberta Agriculture. "The handful of unsatisfied have usually neglected quality or design standards, or encountered an extraordinary coyote which must be removed."

Field fencing seldom keeps a coyote away from livestock because it will usually go under or through the fence. Good quality electric fencing, on the other hand, will protect most livestock. A report by Ross Hall, Department of Natural Resources, Nova Scotia, recommends a fence that produces enough voltage to overcome the insulation resistance of a coyote's long hair and hide. They add, a minimum charge of 2000 volts is required, and 4000-5000 volts may work much better.

Guard dogs have been known to protect livestock from coyotes. However, it must be a dog that has a fondness for the livestock and a disliking for the coyote. Many dogs will suffice if raised with livestock. Some ranchers have turned to llamas and donkeys to protect their sheep, and studies have indicated that sheep losses are lower when llamas stayed with the sheep.

The best way to deal with a potential nuisance coyote is to prevent a problem before it occurs. If no other options are available, however, trapping or killing the coyote may become necessary. This is particularly true once the coyote has fed upon livestock or poultry or has bypassed or beaten another system used to protect livestock and poultry.

In states or provinces where coyotes are classified as predators, there is a possibility that you can kill or remove them any time. However, if the state/province considers the coyote a furbearing game animal, you may be limited to trapping or killing the coyote only during a designated season, or perhaps not at all. First check with a wildlife agency before trapping or killing a coyote.

A carefully placed bait may attract coyotes. I have used fresh meat scraps to attract them during the hunting seasons, starting with about 30 to 40 pounds. A large dose of bait will keep you from making regular visitations to the bait, and in the process reduce human scent in the area. But when I do visit the bait site and replenish it, I make it a point to wear knee-high rubber boots with my pants tucked into the boots. Unlike leather footwear that may leave human scent, rubber boots leave little or no human scent behind. The coyote's keen sense of smell cannot be overlooked. Once it has detected your presence, it may not return to the bait.

A bait that coyotes have hit for two or three weeks steadily can usually be hunted. Early mornings and late afternoons provide the best opportunities for hunting. It is important to select an ambush location where the wind blows from the bait to you.

Most coyote trappers rely on old road beds, logging roads or trails since coyotes frequently use these routes for travel. No. 3 or 4 leghold traps are recommended. It is also important to set several traps near the location where damage has occurred. Finally, place traps just off the sides of the coyote's travel route where the wind will blow the lure towards the trail.

The coyote poses additional threats to man that do not involve the loss of livestock and poultry. They have been known to sneak into the suburbs and kill pets near homes. This has occurred frequently in California. Coyotes can also carry rabies. With this in mind, many have come to despise the coyote. However, this predator is one of North America's most intellectual hunters that adapts to almost every type of habitat. He deserves our respect and a place for tomorrow.

Foxes

Although the canine family includes four species of foxes, the gray and red foxes are the most widespread. The gray fox prefers dense and rugged terrain, though it sometimes appears in farmland regions. It inhabits most of the 48 contiguous states. The red fox often lives around the fringes where grasslands and farmlands meet woodlands, but it has shown up in heavily forested areas. Its range is much more widespread than the gray fox. It is found in all of the provinces of Canada, and in most of the United States, including Alaska. About the only place where you will not find the red fox is in the remote desert states of the Southwest.

True, the fox is very sly, preferring not to show his true identity whenever possible. However, this nocturnal predator has become a nuisance in many urban and rural areas. Gray and red foxes

Figure 5-5. Fox tracks will be smaller and more rounded than the tracks of a coyote. Illus. by Larry Smail.

have caused a multitude of problems for some people, simply because these canines cannot pass up an easy meal. Poultry and sometimes small pets become an easy meal. Once these canines have discovered a free handout, they will not hesitate to come back for more.

There is little difference in size of the gray and red fox, though the mature red fox may weigh a pound or two more than the gray fox. Either may weigh up to 10 pounds, but they are easily distinguished by their colors. Gray foxes tend to have light or dark gray fur, while the fur of red foxes ranges from a rust color to almost blond.

The diet of gray and red foxes is about the same, though red foxes usually kill poultry and livestock more often than gray. Both eat their share of songbirds and game birds, as well as mice, moles, chipmunks, hares and rabbits, squirrels and a variety of other rodents and small mammals. Foxes will also eat food that they do not kill.

The gray fox is not made for long-distance runs such as the red fox. Perhaps this has something to do with why it spends more time in its den than the red fox. However, both

Figure 5-6. There is more space between the pads of a mink track than in the pads of a fox track. Illus. by Larry Smail.

predators hunt almost every day of their life. Their keen senses also see to it that starvation will not be a factor, even when Old Man Winter arrives.

The tracks of the gray fox seldom exceed one and one half inches in length, though the track of a red fox may be two inches in length. However, the tracks of both canines are somewhat rounded and not as oval shaped as the track of a coyote (Figure 5-5). Because of the numerous hairs on the feet, the pads of the fox's feet do not show as much detail as other canines even when they have walked across snow.

It is primarily poultry raisers who have problems with foxes. Foxes will climb as well as squeeze through tight openings when a meal is just on the other side. Thus, chickens, ducks, geese, guineas and turkeys are at risk unless you take necessary precautions to protect them from foxes. Livestock farmers also suffer occasional losses of lambs and small pigs when a hungry fox begins prowling.

During a six-month period (October to March), I lost five of six turkeys to predators. The turkeys were kept in a large enclosure with white-tailed deer. The killings began at night but the predators eventually began rampaging during the daylight hours. I finally determined that foxes killed four of the turkeys. The other, a gobbler that I had raised for almost six years, fell victim to a coyote.

When foxes kill poultry they usually bite the animal's head and neck first. However, poultry killed by minks can resemble a fox kill since they also bite the neck and head of their prey. The mink track is somewhat different and smaller than the track of a fox (Figure 5-6). After the kill, the fox will usually tear into flanks or ribs of the animal. However, they can leave quite a mess and make it difficult to determine what predator killed a particular animal. When foxes kill large turkeys, you may find trails of blood and feathers strung over a sizable area. This occurs because they may have difficulty killing a 25-pound bird immediately. If left undisturbed after the kill, though, they may bury portions of the carcass that they could not eat right away.

I once saw a red fox feeding on my turkey only minutes after it had killed the bird. The fox saw me and promptly vanished into a nearby grown-up field. I returned to the house and grabbed my rifle, then set up 60 yards from the downed turkey to wait on the fox. It took less than 10 minutes for the fox to return to claim his kill. Moments later I was carrying both the fox and turkey out of the field.

If you have identified a fox as killing livestock or poultry, it may be possible that you can legally trap or kill the animal. Most states and provinces consider the fox a furbearer and game animal. However, check the regulations of your local wildlife agency before taking action. Many may only allow the taking of fox during special seasons. Others may allow you to kill or remove a fox during closed seasons when the fox depredates on your property.

I have not had much luck baiting foxes. Coyotes and foxes do not get along and a coyote will make it a point to keep a fox away from a bait. In fact, coyotes often kill foxes.

You might also consider calling a nuisance fox into gun range. As is with most predators, the fox may find it hard to resist the squeals of a cottontail rabbit, or perhaps the squeals of a mouse or songbird. Several game call companies manufacture easy-to-use predator calls and cassette tapes to lead you through the calling fundamentals. Most calls sell for less than $10.

Complete camouflage is necessary when calling to a shrewd fox, or a coyote for that matter. That includes the hands and face. Before calling, set up against a solid background, such as a large tree or dense brush, to help you blend with your surroundings. I would also suggest you set up where you have a good view of the terrain. Skilled predator hunters use high-powered rifles (if legal), small caliber rifles and shotguns.

Trapping is a more effective method of controlling a nuisance fox, simply because the trap can work 24 hours per day. However, since foxes can be difficult to lure into a trap, many professional

The author used a snare to remove a red fox that had consistently killed poultry for several weeks. Photo by Vikki L. Trout

trappers use a "dirt hole set." This consists of digging a small hole in an area that a fox frequently travels through (fence rows, old road beds and fields), or near areas where depredation occurs. You should place traps about 40 or 50 yards upwind from where you expect the fox to be. Most trappers select upwind locations since it may keep dogs from finding the trap. The nose of the fox, though, will have no difficulty locating the set. The fox will not shy away if you use rubber gloves and wear rubber boots while setting the trap.

A No. 2 coil spring trap will work well. After digging a hole just a little larger than the trap, drive a steel stake into the ground to secure the trap. Then place the trap and set it, covering it with a small piece of wax paper or wire screen. Using a sifter, sift the dirt that you removed when the hole was dug to cover the trap, keeping your set level. Using a fox lure (available from a trapping supply house), place a few drops of the lure on a small bedding of natural foliage a few inches from the trap. I would also suggest you re-place the lure after a rain.

You might also consider a snare to catch a problem fox. This consists of a wire that tightens as a fox passes through a loop made from the wire. On one occasion, I used a snare to take a fox that had killed a few of my turkeys.

Frightening devices are seldom effective once a fox has fed on poultry. I once chased a red fox, yelling at it and throwing rocks. He returned a couple of days later at midday. The best way to control a nuisance fox and protect poultry is with net wire fenc-ing. Closing them up at night does not offer total protection since a fox will often prey on poultry in the daylight hours.

We must respect the intelligence of the fox. In fact, even the professional trapper admires this mischievous, cunning predator. We may outsmart one or two here and there, but you can bet that there is another that will always be one step ahead of our next move.

Mountain Lion

Cougar and puma are common names given to the mountain lion. The huge cat is primarily a nocturnal hunter, and for good reason. The mountain lion's eyes allow him to see well in the dark hours. His second best sense is his sense of smell.

The mountain lion's shyness plays a significant role in the solitary, nocturnal life he portrays. I know of many individuals who have lived in "cat country" their entire lives without ever spot-ting one of the great beasts. During the last three decades, I have spent many days and nights in the backcountry of the Northwest-ern states where the mountain lion thrives. However, I have seen them only on one occasion. My sighting occurred in northern Idaho early one morning as I drove a road in the high country, two years before the writing of this book began. Two mountain lions, prob-ably a male and female, stood less than 20 yards from my vehicle for just a few brief seconds. The sighting, however, made my trip worthwhile. Since that day, after hiking into remote mountainous regions, I have heard others "screaming."

The mountain lion is commonly found in the western provinces of Canada and in the western states from Alaska to Arizona. Mexico also has a growing number of the big cats. Though once extinct in the Eastern states, it has now rebounded in the Appalachian mountain regions, and within the boundaries of a few of the southernmost states.

Though they prefer rugged rocky country, the mountain lion also inhabits many brushy areas. Wherever prey is available, they will not hesitate to set up residence nearby. It is not uncommon for them to travel up to 20 miles in one night.

Figure 5-7. The retractable claws will not show in the track of a mountain lion, even though it is much larger than the track of a bobcat or lynx. Illus. by Larry Smail.

Identifying a mountain lion is not difficult since it is the largest of all wild cats in North America other than the spotted jaguar found in Mexico. The mountain lion may grow to a length of eight feet or more and weigh up to 180 pounds. Adult males commonly weigh 30 pounds more than females of the same age. The hide of the cat can range from a rusty appearance to a dull gray or tan. Both the yellow eyes and long tail (30 inches or more) are dead giveaways.

You can also locate scent posts in areas the mountain lion inhabits. These are small mounds of dirt scratched up by the cougar so that it can urinate in the fresh soil.

The tracks of a mountain lion are much larger than those of their cousins, the bobcat and lynx. The adult cougar leaves behind a track about four to four and a half inches wide and about four inches long. When running, the tracks may be spaced apart by four feet or more. As is with other felines, the claws are retractable and do not show in the tracks (Figure 5-7).

Deer make up much of the mountain lion's carnivorous diet. These big cats can patiently and quietly stalk and kill them. Mountain lions possess an enormous amount of strength and kills promptly by biting the back of the deer's neck. It is also not uncommon to find claw marks along the back of an animal killed by the mountain lion. It also eats a variety of other mammals, both small and large, often covering all or portions of what they do not eat with dirt, twigs and leaves. A grizzly bear commonly covers its leftovers as well, and may fool those that have discovered the covered carcass. However, grizzly bears, and black bears for that matter, feed on carrion while the mountain lion usually prefers to kill its prey.

Livestock losses due to mountain lions have been quite

The mountain lion is a shy animal but has been responsible for many human deaths.

significant. The USDA reported that mountain lions killed more than 8,000 head of calves/cattle in 1995, and more than 28,000 lambs/sheep and goats in 1994. In Rio Blanco County, Colorado during the month of June 1994, mountain lions killed 107 lambs and one adult sheep over a period of five nights. ADC specialists caught two lions within 12 days to resolve the problem. However, among the predators that prey upon livestock, the mountain lion ranks far below the coyote.

Many ranchers who have suffered livestock losses have not hesitated to remove dense foliage near their livestock since cougars often utilize brushy areas to remain hidden. Electric fences may also deter mountain lions. And according to ADC officials, the Electronic Guard (a strobe light/siren device) made by USDA/APHIS/ADC, may also keep the cats from attacking livestock.

Mountain lions sometimes attack people. California has most definitely seen its share of tragedies. A four-year-old girl was attacked in March 1986 by a mountain lion in Caspers State Park, leaving her blind in one eye and partially paralyzed. A nine-year-old boy suffered from many puncture wounds that required 600 stitches after he was attacked in March 1992 at Gaviota State Park. An El Dorado County woman was killed by a mountain lion in April 1994 while jogging. In December 1994, a mountain lion killed a woman while she walked in Cuyamaca State Park.

There are many more incidents in North America than those I mentioned but they make the point. The mountain lion can pose a threat to human lives. Unfortunately, human and lion confrontations could also increase significantly in the years ahead. Hunting bans that have stopped mountain lion hunting in some states could play a major role in the growing number of mountain lions and potential confrontations with man in the future. I should add, in California where the ban stopped hunting in 1990, officials found it necessary to kill 11 mountain lions that were thought to be a threat to public safety in California during 1994.

It has been said that "action" commonly attracts the mountain lion. A person jogging and children playing and running may actually entice the cougar to pursue the individual. Whenever you plan to spend time in mountain lion habitat, it will help to stay in groups. Children should never be allowed to roam on their own. A lone individual is much more susceptible than two or more people.

Mountain lions have also attacked and killed pets when opportunity allowed. California wildlife officials tracked down a cougar in 1995 after it had carried off a large Labrador-pit bull that survived the attack. Officials also blamed the same mountain lion for killing two dogs in the area earlier that year. It was reported that the big cat may have lost its fear of people, or perhaps it found it easier to feed on domestic dogs than wild animals.

Hunting is often the answer to controlling nuisance mountain lions. They are usually tracked with good hounds. Though a cougar can easily kill most dogs used for hunting them, it will not hesitate to go up a tree when necessary to avoid dogs. Before killing a mountain lion, though, you should know the regulations. In many areas the mountain lion is fully protected; in other areas the mountain lion can be hunted only during a designated season.

At one time bounties were placed on mountain lions, but that led to a great reduction of these mighty beasts. Fortunately, today, the cougar has made a comeback and has become widespread across North America, partially because it has become a sport animal in some states and provinces, regulated by wildlife officials.

Raccoons

Many people in the suburbs and rural areas have enjoyed making pets of raccoons, though it may be illegal to do so without a special permit. But these cute, cuddly furbearers have caused a variety of problems, even in urban districts. They will sometimes kill poultry and other farm-raised animals. They will also take advantage of pets, and both domestic and wild ducks. One Indiana study showed raccoons were responsible for raiding several nests and eating the eggs of wood ducks. They also destroy wild turkey

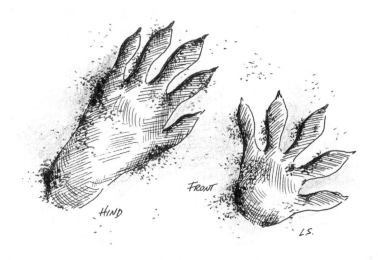

Figure 5-8. The hind foot of a raccoon is longer than the front. The tracks of a raccoon resemble that of the skunk. Illus. by Larry Smail.

nests and eat the eggs when opportunity strikes.

Raccoons are found within the boundaries of all the lower 48 states, and in the southern portions of many provinces in Canada. They adapt to a variety of habitats, from low-lying marshes to high-ridge woodlands, but raccoons usually prefer to be near water.

Known as the animal that wears the black mask, the raccoon varies in color from gray to reddish-brown. It also has several unmistakable black rings on the tail. Adult raccoons commonly weigh 20 pounds or more. These nocturnal tree dwellers prefer to lie amongst the limbs or den in hollow trees during the daylight hours, feeding and traveling primarily at night. They are not true hibernators, though they move less in the cold winter months than they do during the spring, summer and fall.

The raccoon's carnivorous diet consists of birds, crayfish, fish, frogs and many small rodents. For this reason it does much of its feeding around water. However it is also omnivorous, eating acorns, fruits and vegetation. I have watched them feed on acorns in towering oaks for hours at a time. Many have claimed that the masked animal washes its food before it eats it, but this is true only some of the time.

Though many animals cause damage to crops, the raccoon, a close relative to the bear, is often the blame. They love corn and will not hesitate to feed on this agricultural handout whenever possible. Unfortunately, for those who have gardens, the raccoon seems to prefer sweet corn over all other varieties. Their damage to a corn crop is often unmistakable. Usually, they will climb up the stalk, often breaking it in half. They also peel back the husks with their finely designed front feet.

You can easily identify tracks of the raccoon since they have five toes on each foot, and longer toes on the hind feet. The track of the front foot resembles a small hand print (Figure 5-8). They also have an unmistakable way of walking flatfooted. Raccoons will occasionally walk along logging roads and trails, defecating on small open surfaces or atop rocks.

Since the raccoon will eat almost anything, it will not hesitate to raid a garbage can. Many believe that metal garbage cans attract them because they are shiny. It is a fact that the curious raccoon is attracted to bright items. Their sense of smell is not superb but their eyes quickly recognize food sources. They can easily turn over unsecured garbage cans and remove the lids with their handlike feet. Some claim they can even remove the lids from jars. Once they have made a habit of feeding on garbage, poultry or in gardens near a home, they will likely set up residence close by. They may even enter an uncapped chimney or use a nearby outbuilding to stay put until dark.

Jerry Joe Barnett, an Indiana trapper for more than 40 years, often works in controlling nuisance animals. He claims that he received far more reports of raccoons damaging property than preying upon poultry. He claims they often tore shingles off roofs or siding from dwellings in an attempt to get inside.

In some areas where raccoons are around people, they lose

fear of them and become dangerous. ADC assistance was requested during 1994 at a park in San Luis Obispo County, California, after raccoons began harassing and biting park visitors. It seems the raccoons also damaged camping equipment while they searched for food. However, ADC officials resolved the problem after they placed cage traps in the area for several nights in a row to capture the hostile animals.

If you have ever visited Cades Cove in the Great Smoky Mountains National Park, you may have seen a raccoon or two along the roadway. Since visitors often feed the raccoons (park officials frown on this), they will not hesitate to approach humans. On one occasion while photographing deer, however, a raccoon came up and began begging for a handout. Once I did not respond to its request, it grabbed the cuff of my pants and snarled furiously. I finally shook the coon from my leg (before it bit me) and left the scene to report the aggressive critter to a park ranger.

Live traps made of heavy wire are often used to remove nuisance raccoons. Once trapped, you should transport the animal several miles from the location of capture.

When raccoons feed on poultry and ducks, they often eat the breasts and leave the entrails nearby. You will sometimes find leftover portions near water though they often eat everything.

Since the raccoon is a furbearing animal, special hunting and trapping seasons have been set in most states/provinces. Raccoons often provide income for trappers and hunters. The prices of their hides have varied over the past couple of decades, from all-time highs to all-time lows. Hunters often use dogs to get raccoons. I might add, some take their hunting seriously, paying thousands of dollars for a qualified hound.

It is often more practical to keep a raccoon away than it is to remove it from a problem area. Electric fencing is particularly beneficial around open gardens. However, overhanging tree limbs will allow the culprit to bypass the hot wire and drop into the garden. Therefore, you should consider removing any overhanging limbs before placing an electric fence.

A hot wire may also keep a raccoon away from poultry. The best prevention is to put the wire at the top of the poultry fence. Then, as the raccoon climbs the field fence, it will come into contact with the hot wire.

Garbage cans should be staked or tied down with metal wire. For the lid of the can, I would suggest you use a wire or stretch cord, placing it over the top of the lid and fastening it to each handle.

If it becomes mandatory to remove a nuisance raccoon, a proper set trap will work almost immediately. Since the raccoon is a very curious animal, live traps (No. 3 or 3A) work well when baited with irresistible foods such as corn, fish, or sweets. However, you must use a sturdy trap. Raccoons are very strong and could tear up a trap made of light wire. Finally, secure the trap with rocks or brush to keep it from tipping.

Leg-hold and Conibear traps may also be effective but you must take into consideration that a pet could become the victim when used in residential areas. A Size 1 ½ leg hold or Size 220 Conibear trap will work effectively when baited with fish. The trapper must use strong stakes, however. Place the trap at points of entry when the problem occurs near buildings.

If you have successfully live-trapped a raccoon, I would recommend you use extreme caution. They may not hesitate to use claws and teeth on a human if they feel it necessary. They could also carry parasites and diseases. Finally, when transporting a raccoon, you should take it a few miles from the trapped location. Otherwise, they could return and cause future problems.

Skunks

Mention the word "skunk" and some people immediately respond negatively. After all, this member of the weasel family is widely known for its ability to defend itself by dispensing a disgusting odor from the anal gland. However, the truth is, the skunk may do more good than harm. Many farmers and gardeners appreciate seeing an occasional skunk since it consumes large numbers of mice, rats and insects.

Figure 5-9. The front foot of the skunk measures about 1 1/2 inches but the oval hind foot may exceed 2 inches. The tracks of a skunk resemble those of the raccoon. Illus. by Larry Smail.

Several species of skunks roam throughout much of North America. The most common are striped and spotted skunks. The striped skunk has set up home within the boundaries of about every state in the lower 48, and north into most provinces of Canada. The range of the spotted skunk is somewhat more limited.

The skunk can survive in a variety of habitats, but the striped skunk in particular prefers habitat that provides a diversity of woodlots, pastures or agriculture lands. They often use hollow logs or underground tunnels dug by other mammals for dens. However, they are not good tree climbers. In the coldest part of the winter they will usually hole up in a den.

The striped skunk is recognized by its white stripes along the back that resemble a large "V," and stripes on the long tail. The spotted skunk is very similar, except that the stripes are continuous lines of spots. Both can have color variations, sometimes primarily black, and others mostly white.

The front and hind tracks of the skunk differ considerably. They have five toes on each foot but the hind feet are almost twice as long as the front feet. The front feet are rounded and the hind feet oval (Figure 5-9). In most cases, you will also see claw marks. If the tracks are not sharp, you could mistake them for raccoon tracks.

As mentioned previously, the skunk is primarily carnivorous, feeding on rodents and insects. However, this nocturnal animal also feeds on some plants, eggs and occasionally carrion. It may even surprise a mammal as large as a cottontail rabbit. Its desire to scavenge on dead animals is one reason why you often see this animal become a road kill. It may travel a roadway in search of a dead animal, and eventually become a victim itself. Skunks living near the suburbs and urban areas will also feed on garbage or handouts.

In some state parks where skunks have lost a fear of people, they often beg for food near campgrounds. Many people remain fearful of getting close to them because they do not want a dose of their disgusting scent. In all reality, though, skunks accustomed to people seldom spray them. But they will not hesitate to discharge their nasty scent if they feel threatened. This is one reason why the skunk seldom worries about predators. The skunk has the ability to spray up to 12 feet, and it can spray several times if necessary.

Damages caused by skunks vary, but one common problem is when they set up home within or near a dwelling. They often get under porches or into basements and barns. This is usually recognized by a consistent odor at the same location (sometimes the odor comes from another animal that a skunk sprayed).

Although they are not notorious killers of poultry, they will occasionally feed on chickens. But if poultry eggs are available, they prefer to eat them. Skunks do not swallow the whole egg, as do snakes. Normally, you will find egg shell remnants whenever the skunk has invaded a poultry house.

Skunks may also carry rabies. For this reason, always avoid contact with a skunk that acts abnormally, and particularly one that appears aggressive. I discuss rabies in further detail in a later chapter.

In most states/provinces, the skunk is not protected. Thus, you can hunt them in these areas with legal methods whenever they become a nuisance.

To prevent a skunk from using a dwelling as a den (they often seek these areas to feed on rodents), close off all crawl spaces. It is vitally important to build a skirt with wood or metal around a mobile home since the skunk will not hesitate to go under them for denning. You will want to make sure the skunk is not in the dwelling when you close off the opening, however.

You can also consider a fence to keep a skunk from entering a crawl space or dwelling. A short fence is effective since skunks cannot climb. Poultry fencing is recommended to keep them from going through a fence. It may also be necessary to sink it into the ground a few inches so they cannot dig under the fence. Some specialists recommend using ammonia soaked rags to discourage skunks. I would also suggest you keep garbage in a container and eliminate excess pet food near dwellings since it can attract skunks.

If it becomes necessary to remove a skunk by trapping, live traps work effectively. Because of odor, leghold traps are not recommended. You can bait live traps with chicken, fish and even a meaty pet food. But you must handle the trap and skunk cautiously when transporting the animal to another location. A concealed wooden live trap will keep the animal from seeing and spraying you. If you use a wire type live trap, consider covering it with a blanket (make sure you don't use a blanket that you cover yourself with every night).

If it becomes necessary to remove skunk odor, visit your veterinarian. He probably has deodorants available to alleviate undesirable odors. Vinegar, baking soda and tomato juice may also work to remove skunk odor from people and pets.

Chapter 6

Hoofed Mammals

Throughout most of North America you will find a distribution of hoofed mammals — bison, deer, caribou, elk, moose, mountain goat, sheep, pronghorn antelope and wild pigs. This chapter focuses on four species that occasionally cause damage to gardens, crops, livestock and other types of personal property.

Most hoofed mammals have a four-part stomach and are considered ruminants. Thus, ruminants have a habit of chewing their cud. When chewing their cud, they actually regurgitate food. Most hoofed animals are also even-toed, meaning they have two or four toes on each foot. Of the hoofed mammals that carry headgear, most shed their antlers in the winter or early spring months. Almost immediately, new antler growth begins. By autumn, the development of the new antlers is complete. Pronghorn antelope are an exception, since they have horns, not antlers. They do not shed their horns.

Surprisingly, over one half of U.S. farms surveyed a few years ago by the National Agricultural Statistics Service reported suffering losses caused by wildlife during a twelve-month period. The most frequently reported cause of damage came from the category

"Hoofed Animals." Hoofed animals caused the most damage in the Great Lakes, Midwest and Northeast regions.

Deer

Of all the deer species in North America, the whitetail is by far the most numerous. At the time of this writing, approximately 25 million white-tailed deer are found in the U.S., Canada and Mexico. Because of the high population of whitetails, I have made them the central point of interest in this section of deer. Black-tailed and mule deer are not as widespread as the whitetail, nor do they create as many problems. The only places you will not find whitetails are the dry regions of the far west.

First, let me say that I have a real attachment to the white-tailed deer. They have provided me with many years of hunting and photography pleasure. A few years ago, I also obtained a special permit to keep them in captivity. The knowledge I have gained from studying their behavior has been very rewarding. To say the least, I have come to love and admire this fine animal.

One reason the whitetail has become so widespread is because it has adapted to various habitats. From the deciduous forests to the farmland regions, it survives and thrives. They can live in bottomlands or mountainous terrain. However, they often prefer the fringes. If they had their choice deer would probably choose a diversity of habitat that includes an even mixture of agricultural lands and timber. This provides them with both cover and food, the two essentials necessary for their survival. But don't think for a moment that the white-tailed deer does not thrive in prairie lands. Even a pocket of brush or timber may provide them with enough cover. In fact, a white-tailed deer can hide in knee-high weeds when necessary. These factors have something to do with why deer thrive close to man. Hunting has even begun within the boundaries of many major metropolitan areas to control whitetail populations.

One reason why deer populations have exploded is because

The white-tailed deer has adapted to our habits. Today it is not uncommon to see them close to the suburbs and urban areas.

of the fine management programs initiated by state and provincial offices and sportsmen's dollars. Game and fish departments have worked hard to make them the No. 1 "big game" animal. Limited seasons and regulated harvests have not caused any serious reductions in deer populations. In most states, increases in populations occur annually. Insurance companies are dismayed by growing numbers of deer/vehicle collisions, and many landowners complain about damages that deer cause. But rest assured, deer are a highly valuable wildlife resource. Hunters spend about $10 billion each year for equipment and services. Their license fees are also taxed to help manage other wildlife species.

There is one major reason why the white-tailed deer continues to flourish. It has amazing senses. Its sense of smell is probably the best, but none of the deer's senses lack in ability. For the hunter, he is bumping heads with one of nature's wisest, and most cunning creatures.

These deer tracks are probably those of a buck. Notice the drag marks in the snow. Except for a deep snow, does seldom leave drag marks.

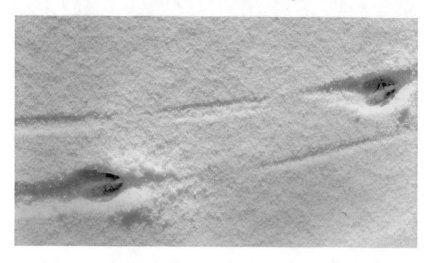

Bucks seldom stay with does until autumn when the breeding begins. The bucks will continue rutting as long as there are does to breed. During the rut, which can last from October through February, depending on location, the bucks will polish their antlers on trees. This also builds neck muscles that may be helpful when fighting with rivals.

The doe stays in estrous for about 28 hours. Once bred, she will carry the fawns for about 200 to 210 days before giving birth. A doe will usually give birth to one fawn her first year, and two each year thereafter. They are born with spots to camouflage them, and no scent. Predators can pass within a few feet and never know the fawn is there. A fawn weighs about 4 to 5 pounds at birth but grows quickly. By age of a year and a half, a well-nourished deer could easily weigh 150 pounds or more. Deer in the southern U.S. tend to be smaller than northern deer, where bucks may reach a weight of 350 pounds or more.

Deer tracks are usually unmistakable. Many people who live in the rural areas and suburbs consistently see their triangular-shaped tracks. As far as I know, we still cannot tell the difference in buck and doe tracks. The size of the track may provide some proof since most bucks are larger than does. In snow you may see drag marks behind the tracks of a buck. A walking doe tends to lift her hoofs a little higher than a buck and seldom leaves drag marks behind the track except in deep snow. When deer run, or when they walk in mud or snow, you may also see the marks of their dew claws (the heel of the hoof) a couple of inches behind the track.

Deer are nocturnal, though we often see them in daylight hours. They are also creatures of habit. They may visit the same food sources and select the same cover to hide in every day, providing these patterns are not interrupted by humans or other predators. But they need several pounds of food each day to survive. Their normal diet consists of acorns, fruits, alfalfa, clover, soybeans, corn, hemlock, fir, maple, honeysuckle and woody plants too numerous to mention. However, unlike cattle that graze, deer browse. In other words, they seldom feed at one spot for a long time.

Deer cause a variety of problems, from personal property damage to crop devastation. They also carry many ticks, of which one causes Lyme disease. I discuss ticks and Lyme disease in a later chapter. As for property and crop damage, the problems are seldom resolved easily.

Several airports have experienced problems with deer. In 1994, two deer were struck by a twin-engine aircraft while it attempted to depart from the Cumberland, Maryland Municipal Airport. ADC investigated the incident and recommended habitat modification, fencing and controlled hunting to reduce the deer population in the area. The two deer caused an estimated damage of $1 million to the aircraft.

Deer also caused two collisions at the Prestonburg, Kentucky Big Sandy Regional Airport recently. A spotlight survey conducted by ADC showed 20 deer near the airport runways. ADC then demonstrated to airport personnel the use of pyrotechnics and provided

Type of Damage	Total Cases
Personal Garden	278
Forage Crop	218
Row Crop	159
Tobacco Beds	100
Orchard	61
Personal Property	46
Commercial Garden	41
Other	38

Table 17. Types of deer damage that occurred in Kentucky, 1994. Source: Kentucky Department of Fish and Wildlife Resources.

the equipment until a deer-proof fence could be installed to solve the problem.

In 1990, a Northwest Airline plane struck a deer, causing minor damage. However, officials claimed they had to do something quickly to guarantee the safety of passengers and airline personnel. They ruled out fences because the airport was located in a low, swampy area. The Florida Department of Natural Resources finally resolved the matter when they issued permits to kill the problem deer. After the hunt, 43 deer had been killed and their meat donated to children's homes.

Deer cause a variety of problems for people in both rural and urban areas. A 1994 Kentucky report showed various categories of deer damage complaints. Damage to "Personal Garden" was listed as the primary complaint about deer (Table 17). Incidentally, Kentucky's deer damage complaints in 1994 had increased 60 percent over the previous year.

Deer eat a variety of home-grown vegetables. I once lost 40 heads of lettuce in one night after several deer invaded my garden only 100 feet from the house. Deer also love to eat bean plants (particularly those of the bush bean type) and sweet corn. Equally damaging when they visit a garden, however, is the destruction they cause to plants they do not eat. They will walk where they please, trampling whatever plants they pass over. I would recommend, though, that you do positively identify deer as the nuisance animal causing garden damage before taking precautions to keep them away. Several animals, including woodchucks (groundhogs),

Deer feed on many types of forage, from woody plants to crops. Landowners suffer losses consistently because of deer damage to both small gardens and agricultural crops.

rabbits and birds also enjoy dining out in a garden. Tracks and droppings will help you determine which of the culprits are guilty. Deer droppings are round or slightly oval and about the size of your little fingernail. They are usually black or very dark green and sometimes clustered in a mass.

Deer also cause damage to fruit trees and ornamentals. When deer feed on twigs, however, they often leave it shredded. This is because they do not have incisors in the upper jaw to bite off a twig cleanly. Rabbits and woodchucks, on the other hand, do make clean bites.

Trees can suffer damage or eventually die after a buck has rubbed his antlers on the trunk of the tree. Bucks begin rubbing trees of various sizes when the rut starts in autumn. Some trees they rub may be one inch or less in diameter, while others may have a diameter the size of your thigh. Deer rub a variety of trees, but cedar, pine, fir and maple are some of their favorites. When a buck rubs its antlers on a tree, it will strip the bark and often gouge it deeply with the tines of the antlers.

There is one recommended way to prevent a rutting buck from rubbing a cherished tree. Take a four-foot piece of flexible, four-inch plastic pipe and cut it down one side. The slit will allow you to spread the pipe and put it around the trunk of the tree. Four feet of pipe should also keep a buck from being able to get to any other part of the tree.

The more deer in a given area, the more potential there is of receiving damage caused by deer. Many state and provincial officials have not found a way of eliminating deer problems except by increasing hunting opportunities and harvests. Some state parks that have not allowed hunting previously now do so to reduce deer herds within their boundaries. This is often necessary because deer tend to have a small home range. They can overbrowse an area, such as state parks that do not allow hunting. This can cause extensive damage to plants (some species of plant life are totally eliminated) and other wildlife species. The deer, meanwhile, may also become undernourished. An unhealthy deer can contract a disease or fall victim to starvation during severe winters.

Trapping deer and transporting them normally is not feasible. One example is Brown County State Park in Indiana. Two dozen individuals spent more than 300 hours in the park and were only able to trap eleven deer. Trapped deer can also die of stress. Contraceptives (there is nothing approved by the Food and Drug Administration) would not offer any immediate relief, and there is no practical way to inject the entire herd of does in a given area. Artificial feeding is also costly, ineffective and may deliver improper management messages to the public.

Fencing may keep problem deer away from gardens and small nurseries. Field fence is usually costly since a height of seven to eight feet would be necessary. Electric fences, though, are not as costly and will serve the same purpose when constructed properly. For the best results, place the wire 18 inches or more off the ground. Deer that attempt to go under the fence will usually be shocked. Some may jump over the wire without touching it, however. For maximum results, you might consider two wires, one about 14 inches and the other 40 inches off the ground. Many specialists, trained in controlling problem deer, recommend that voltage be 4000 or higher.

Specialists also recommend using peanut butter to attract deer to an electric fence. They suggest wrapping small pieces of aluminum foil ribbons to the fence and smearing peanut butter onto the foil. Deer are attracted to peanut butter and may not hesitate to touch it with their nose or mouth, thus receiving a shock.

Before installing an electric fence, ask yourself if the damage warrants the cost. For instance, last year I tried using human hair around my garden. I had heard that it worked and would cost nothing other than my time invested in obtaining the hair and spreading it. To start, I used a grocery sack of hair obtained from barber shops. I spread the hair completely around the garden (some use mesh bags filled with hair and tie them around the garden). The technique worked for about 10 days. After a couple of good rains, the hair no longer kept deer from entering the garden. I have also heard of hanging bar soaps around a garden but have yet to try this method to control problem deer.

Noise devices are usually ineffective. Deer become used to most sounds, such as gunshots, firecrackers and siren devices. A dog fastened up nearby may discourage deer, but this is only a temporary solution. Once the deer realize the dog cannot reach them, it will no longer keep them away. I would suggest that you not allow a dog to roam freely, since it could lead to other problems (it could also be illegal).

For both large and small gardens (40 acres or less), along with nurseries and orchards, you might consider a newer type of electric fence called Polytape. Polytapes are plastic ribbons about one-half inch wide, interwoven with fine strands of stainless steel or aluminum wire. It is recommended that you suspend Polytape about 30 inches above the ground and electrify it with a low impedance fence charger. Deer can easily jump over such a fence, but its high visibility encourages them to approach the fence with caution and touch it with their nose out of curiosity. The fence easily shows up in low-light conditions. Contact your local hardware and lawn/garden shops to purchase Polytape.

Agricultural crop damage caused by deer continues to increase annually in many states. For instance, Charles Ruth, Deer Project Supervisor for the South Carolina Department of Natural Resources, said the state has seen a corresponding increase in complaints. "The actual number of complaints for agricultural crop depredation has increased from only a few in the early to mid 1980s to over 1,200 in 1995," explained Ruth.

Deer eat a variety of agricultural crops. Corn, soybeans, alfalfa and clover are crops they can severely damage quickly. However, be aware that you can blame damage caused by other animals on deer. A group of hungry wild pigs can devastate an acre or two of corn overnight. They knock over and break the stalks whereas deer simply eat the corn off the stalks.

Some landowners may blame deer for eating soybeans when woodchucks are responsible. The damage caused by each is easily determined, however. When deer feed on soybean plants, they move consistently, biting the top of a plant here and there. When a ground-hog feeds in a soybean field, it will do its dirty work in a small given area. A busy woodchuck may bite the tops of every soybean plant in a radius 50 yards or more.

Lure crops are seldom effective for eliminating prime crop damage. Some landowners have tried to plant attractive lure crops but this usually ends up becoming a costly method that actually draws more deer into the area.

Since deer are a sport animal and may be legally hunted, any landowner suffering from major crop damage should allow ethical sportsmen hunting rights. This is no doubt the most effective way to control crop damage. Regular season harvests may or may not eliminate a problem, however. This will depend upon the number of deer and how effectively they are hunted.

Many states issue out-of-season permits that allow landown-ers, or individuals they appoint, to shoot deer causing damage to crops. After doing a field inspection a district biologist will decide whether or not you can harvest deer, and the number of deer that can be harvested. The only problem I have with killing problem deer is the time of year that some states allow depredation to begin. Some permit this as early as July, before fawns are weaned.

Though wild deer sometimes attack people, these incidents are rare. In fact, captive deer are responsible for most attacks. A captive rutting buck can be dangerous if it has lost its fear of people.

Only a few months before completing this chapter, a cap-tive buck attacked a friend of mine. The victim had raised the buck in an enclosure near his home for more than three years. The buck has always been a fine pet but one day it came up from behind him and suddenly began tossing him around. The deer could have eas-ily killed this person but he came out of the ordeal with no damage beyond several stitches in his thigh and face.

A Texas individual died in 1990 from a crushed skull and several wounds after a buck attacked. It was reported that the man had more than 100 hoof and puncture wounds on his body. The deer was standing beside him when authorities came upon the scene hours later. A deputy shot the buck when it charged him.

I believe, as do many others, that deer in and around urban and rural areas provide us with exciting opportunities. They are beautiful animals that can render us wildlife viewing at its best. We are fortunate they have adapted to our busy world and are capable of surviving in our backyards.

Elk

In 1900, fewer than 100,000 elk (also known as the wapiti) roamed in North America. Today, estimates indicate about one million elk are found in the Rocky Mountains of the U.S. and Canada. Several small bands of elk have been transplanted into Michigan, New York, South Dakota and other states that have suitable habitat. This success story is greatly due to proper wildlife management, sportsmen's dollars and the Rocky Mountain Elk Foundation.

A bull elk is the second largest antlered animal, next to a bull moose. It is because of their size and need to consume several pounds of food each day that some elk become a problem animal. An adult cow can weigh 400 to 500 pounds, while an adult bull may tip the scales at 700 to 800 pounds. There are records of elk weighing much more.

During the winter months, the elk's brown hide is plush with long hairs. As summer approaches, though, they lose the thick hide and develop a thinner rust-colored coat. Their blond rump is unmistakable. Elk are nocturnal, but hunger and cool temperatures may prompt them to feed long after dawn and well before dusk.

My favorite time to see elk begins in mid-September. Each

year, I travel to Yellowstone National Park to photograph the elk and watch the courtship. The rut is truly a sight to behold. Large-antlered bulls round up their harem of cows and bugle consistently to let rivals know that they are king. Some bulls may gather 30 or more cows and calves. They will breed every female that comes into estrous if another bull does not interfere.

The elk has several finely tuned senses but its sense of smell is best. They use their nose to identify predators and food. However, when several elk visit an open area where visibility is good, they rely on their eyes to spot danger.

Elk carry their young a little longer than deer. Most calves are born within 240 days of conception. Adult cows normally have only one calf. The calves, who move little their first few days, are well protected. Simply said, a cow with a calf is nothing to fool with. A mother elk will not tolerate any animal, or man, that appears to be a threat to her youngster.

Elk tracks are much like deer except that they are larger and

Many Yellowstone National Park elk make a habit of feeding on lawns in residential areas at Mammoth. However, tourists and park employees would never call them nuisance animals. The elk are a welcome sight to all.

more rounded. An adult elk track is about four inches long, whereas the track of a calf is about two inches long. However, since the tracks of cattle resemble elk, a better indication of elk may be their droppings. They resemble deer droppings but are about twice the size.

There are other signs that elk may leave behind. Bulls often rub large trees during the rut. It is also common for a small herd to cause considerable damage to landscapes once they have spent a few days feeding.

Preferred elk habitat consists of heavily forested areas interspersed with meadows. During the summer they spend their time in the high elevations. But when Old Man Winter knocks at the door, they usually migrate to lower elevations.

Elk feed primarily on grasses, conifers and berries. Where they have been introduced in the Midwest and East, they also feed on deciduous trees. When elk bite twigs and plants, they rip them, leaving jagged edges. They often cause problems, though, when they compete with horses and cattle for food as they invade pastures. They also take advantage of some crops, damage fences and trample spring and early summer growth.

A Minnesota survey conducted in 1989 showed that 14 states reported damage caused by elk. They included Arkansas, Arizona, Colorado, Idaho, Kansas, Michigan, Minnesota, Montana, New Mexico, Nevada, Oregon, Pennsylvania, Utah and Wyoming. Many of these states categorized species causing damage by including elk with other hoofed mammals, such as antelope and moose. The survey listed damage caused by elk in order of importance. Twelve of the states reported damage to forage and/or row crops as the most common problem. The other two states claimed that damage occurred most often to harvested hay and grain. Other complaints included damage to fences, orchards, tree farms and ornaments. Each state receives technical assistance and some receive loans and/or funding to cope with problems caused by elk.

No doubt, damage to crops and pastures is often minor because elk do not stay put long. Unlike deer with a home range of one or two miles, elk may move several miles. For this reason, most damages are seasonal. The extent of damage during a season depends on available nutrition. Many plants that begin to flourish in the spring will attract elk. In the winter months when food sources dwindle, elk will not hesitate to feed on harvested hay.

For electric fences to work, elk must see them easily. A herd of elk can quickly demolish an electric fence if they are not aware of its presence. Specialists recommend tying bright ribbons to the fence. And, as recommended for deer, peanut butter smeared on strips of foil will prompt an elk to receive a shock. To have an effective electric fence, use several strands of tensile wire so that you will have a height of several feet. High voltage is also necessary. When only field fencing is used, a height of 8 to 10 feet is recommended, with a couple of stands of barbed wire spaced about 6 inches apart at the top of fence. Elk are good jumpers and will readily go over smaller fences when food is on the other side.

When protecting hay, some landowners totally surround it with wooden panels. Frightening devices seldom work on elk and, at best, provide only temporary relief.

Some ranchers also plant lure fields of grasses. This may attract elk and keep them away from pastures and crops.

Small herds of problem elk have been trapped and relocated successfully. It is costly, but effective. In other situations, landowners are sometimes issued permits to kill problem elk. However, some sportsman do not agree to depredating nuisance elk. Many, myself included, believe the elk's No. 1 enemy is starvation. For this reason, I do not relish the idea of depredating nuisance elk when other solutions are available.

Moose

Moose inhabit the provinces of Canada from east to west, and several states in the U.S. where suitable habitat exists. The Alaska-Yukon moose is typically found in portions of Alaska and the Yukon Territory. The Canada moose roams throughout every province of Canada, several northeastern states and the northern portions of many Midwestern states. The Wyoming moose, often called Shiras, inhabits most of the Rocky Mountain states south of the Canadian border. There is little difference in each race, however. Moose are the largest antlered mammals in North America and are seldom mistaken for any other animal. They can easily be identified by their long legs, black or dark brown bodies and sagging bellies.

Though an adult cow moose may weigh several hundred pounds, it does not compare to a large bull. A bull can reach 6 ½ to 7 feet in height and weigh up to 1,500 pounds. The antlers of a mature bull can weigh as much as 100 pounds.

Unlike elk that may travel many miles, moose seldom leave their home range when food is available. They do seek lower elevations when Old Man Winter goes on a rampage in the mountains, however. The moose has a great advantage when it comes to deep snow. Its long legs allow it to browse on twigs that other animals cannot reach.

A powerful bull moose will fight off a rival when the rut begins. During September and October he cares little about feeding and mostly about breeding. He can also be dangerous to man during the rut. Cows with calves have also attacked people. More about that in a moment.

Most calves are born in the late spring. Like many hoofed mammals, a cow moose will usually have one youngster the first year she breeds and two each year thereafter. A moose calf can weigh 25 pounds or more but grows quickly. After only a few days, the calf may be introduced to swimming.

Moose feed on a variety of foods, primarily during the dark hours. They dearly love willow, white birch, fir, aspen, elder and cottonwood. They also eat a variety of pond grasses, weeds, and water lilies. Their fondness for some aquatic vegetation is one reason why we often see them in or near water.

Moose sign can be identified easily. Due to their size and weight, moose cannot help but leave tracks (about 10 inches long from the front tip of the toe to the dew claw) wherever they go. They also leave distinct trails if they visit a food source daily. And if they spend time near these foods, they will leave behind large beds. The scat of moose is in the form of elongated pellets, similar to those of deer and elk. However, moose scat is much larger and usually tan in color. Moose droppings could measure 1 ½ inches long. Moose will also strip the bark of many trees as they feed. Finally, you may also find large rubbed trees when the bulls polish their antlers during the rut.

Surprisingly, moose sometimes become a nuisance. The same Minnesota survey mentioned a few pages ago showed that seven states reported damage caused by moose. The primary cause of damage was not limited to one type, however. Alaska claimed that moose often damaged trees and shrubs. Connecticut listed automobile damage as a major complaint, while Massachusetts said damage to livestock had become the most common problem. Other problems caused by moose included damage to crops and grain.

A report titled "*Resolving Common Moose Problems in New Hampshire*" showed the most common problem was moose walking through fences, resulting in livestock escaping or sustaining injuries. The state also reported problems such as browsing on shrubs, fruit trees or Christmas trees; trampling damage to gardens, lawns and golf courses; nuisance curiosity situations in residential areas; collisions with automobiles. However, the report also said that moose problems are often of limited duration. Many times no action is required other than patience and effective communication with residents.

Most of New Hampshire's problems occur from May to October. According to the NH Cooperative Animal Damage Control Program, it is during the summer months that yearlings disperse and moose are changing their habitat. In the fall, the mating season has much to do with moose causing problems.

Only a few states and provinces receive complaints about moose. Primary damage is to autos, fences, crops, shrubs and gardens.

Newfoundland reports that beavers and moose cause the bulk of nuisance animal situations in the province. According to Mac Pitcher, Animal Curator, moose create problems for many crop farmers. Most of the damages are addressed by directing the hunter harvest to chronic problem areas and permitting farmers to destroy moose which will be claimed by licensed hunters wishing to fill their tags.

Moose are a highly recognized big game animal throughout North America, and its tasty meat (often compared to beef) is greatly relished. Moose populations have also increased significantly in many populated areas. This has played some part in the number of nuisance moose complaints, and the increase of harvests in some states and provinces.

Moose often break down short fences because they don't see them. Highly visible (flag them with bright ribbon) electric fences are recommended around pastures where hay and livestock are found. The New Hampshire report mentioned previously suggests baiting the fence with salt. It claims that attaching metal pot-scrub-bers stuffed with salt-soaked rags to live wires will attract moose, thus shocking them on the nose or mouth. Peanut butter placed on aluminum foil flags (as mentioned previously for deer and elk) will also work effectively when attached to an electric fence about five feet off the ground. Similar techniques requiring less fencing are practical when you need to protect trees and shrubs.

If you consider the weight of a moose, and then imagine running into one with a vehicle, it is easy to understand that an accident could be fatal to both moose and driver. Once in Ontario, I came across a motorcycle in the middle of a narrow road about one hour after dark. The wheels were still turning, and I assumed that someone had lost control of the bike moments before I arrived. Within seconds, I heard the agonizing groans of a man lying on his back near the side of the road. The man claimed he had just hit a moose. Fortunately, he was apparently thrown between the legs of the moose, and escaped serious injury. His motorcycle, though, was totaled.

Moose attacks on people are rare, but they do occur. Alaska reported 45 attacks and maulings in 1995 from moose and bears. Bear were responsible for many of the attacks, but moose accounted for some. In one case, a moose with a calf kicked a 71-year-old man to death on the campus of the University of Alaska. However, reports indicated the moose had been harassed by other individuals just before the attack occurred.

Problems with man often occur when moose pass through urban areas. However, if left alone and given space, they will usu-ally go about their business and retreat to nearby cover. Moose should always be viewed from vehicles or buildings, and never fed or approached. They can attack quickly and without warning.

The harvesting of moose is carefully regulated in every state and province where they are hunted, but the destruction of moose habitat is a familiar sight in some areas. We have carefully transplanted moose in areas where desirable habitat exists, and we are fortunate that moose readily adapt to man.

Wild Pigs

We have a few varieties of wild pigs in the U.S. In the South-west you find the smaller peccaries, or javelina as many call them. In many states from the Midwest to the Atlantic coast, the Euro-pean pig (native to Europe and Asia) roams freely. Wild pigs are also found in California. Many believe wild pigs were first intro-duced by individuals stocking private game preserves.

European wild pigs have expanded into many areas in recent years. They cause many problems on public and private lands, probably because they are nearly impossible to eliminate. A well-nourished sow may have two litters a year and produce 10 or more piglets each time.

Wild pigs were never seen in Indiana until the early 1990s. However, by 1997 a population of wild pigs had expanded into several southern counties of the state. Biologists are very con-cerned about their introduction, and the problems that could occur in the future. No one knows how they got into the state, but offi-cials fear the European pigs are there to stay.

Domestic pigs that have escaped from pig farmers, or were released by individuals to breed with wild pigs, have become com-mon in some areas. Feral pigs are easily distinguished from wild European pigs, however. Feral pigs come in various colors, but the true European pig is usually a dull black or dark brown when it matures. Wild pigs also have longer snouts and legs, and their hair is more bristly and longer than the feral pig. The young wild pigs have a rust-colored hide with black stripes.

Wild pigs prefer dense vegetation. For this reason, they avoid vast farming regions and prairies. Marshes are particularly attrac-tive to wild pigs when they have access to thick brush and hard-woods nearby. They often wallow in swamps to cool off in the summer months.

Adult pigs may weigh several hundred pounds. One wild pig

I harvested field-dressed at 275 pounds. That pig supplied my family with 158 pounds of delicious meat. A wild pig that has fed well for a few years could easily weigh 400 or more pounds.

Male wild pigs grow tusks. These tusks can reach a length of eight inches or more, and come in very handy if the pig is under threat from a predator. Many humans have even been attacked by wild hogs. Though most wild pigs will run away from people, you should not take an angry boar lightly.

We must understand that wild pigs compete with various game animals for food. Wild pigs eat acorns, hickory nuts, walnuts and pecans. Roots are a prime food source when other foods are not available. The wild pig also eats invertebrates and carrion. And when cornfields are available and left undisturbed, they may spend several hours in one location feeding on corn.

Wild pigs often devastate crop fields because they travel in groups. Three or more pigs wreak havoc on a cornfield in a brief period of time. They will crush the stalks to get to the corn and not stop until they have satisfied themselves.

Rooting is another serious problem for many landowners. Wild pigs commonly dig holes, sometimes two or three feet in diameter, as they search for roots or grub. We often find their holes in pastures and crop fields, as well as in hardwood forests. Their rooting destroys plant life and crops and creates hazards for livestock. In many areas, rooting has caused serious erosion problems. Those with gardens seldom suffer minor losses once pigs have found them. In fact, wild pigs can destroy a reasonable size garden in one night. Some specialists have also claimed that wild pigs will invade poultry pens. However, poultry feed is what usually attracts them. Finally, wild pigs can also carry diseases that they can deliver to livestock.

The track of a wild pig resembles that of deer, except they are more rounded on the outer sides of the toes. Another difference is in the dew claws. The dew claws of a wild pig are to the sides of their two toes, whereas on deer they are almost directly behind the

Figure 6-1. The track of the European wild pig. Notice how the dew claws extend beyond the hoof on each side.

hoof (Figure 6-1). European wild pig scat does not resemble deer, elk or moose, however. Scat piles are black, dark green or brown depending on the pig's diet, is sometimes solid but may break into irregular shaped cubes up to one inch in diameter.

Before killing nuisance wild pigs, contact your state fish and game department. They can advise you as to the legal status of removing problem pigs. Some states consider a wild pig a game animal that you can hunt only during seasons. However, depredation permits may be permitted in some areas where damage occurs. In other areas, such as Indiana where I reside, the wild pig is not protected.

If you do attempt to kill nuisance wild pigs, you have a job ahead of you. The wild pig's sense of smell is second to nothing. Hunters often use dogs, but those pigs that seldom come into contact with man become very scrupulous. You may consider baiting,

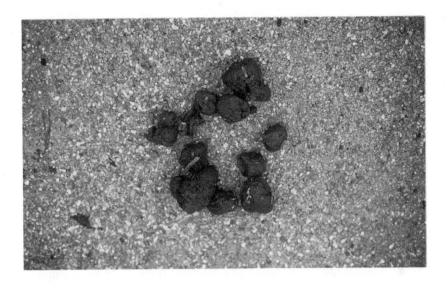

European wild pig scat does not closely resemble the scat of other hoofed animals.

however, if the law permits. I would suggest you wear rubber boots when the baiting begins so the pigs will not be aware of your presence. Rubber boots leave far less human scent behind than do leather boots.

You will probably have more success baiting pigs in the winter months when food sources dwindle. Most pigs are baited with shelled corn or trimmings from a butcher shop. Either can work but both has its pros and cons. Corn has little smell to attract pigs until they are close to the bait. Butcher scraps, on the other hand, have more smell and will attract pigs from longer distances. However, meat, fat and bones will also attract predators which may deter pigs from visiting your bait site regularly.

One major factor to consider when baiting is the quantity of food you provide. You must keep plenty of food on the bait to keep them regular. On a bait site I once opened, 50 pounds of corn could not satisfy them more than two days. For this reason, one could consider the cost of the corn impractical. Wild pigs are also nocturnal, for the most part, and may refuse to come into a bait during daylight hours.

To protect gardens from wild pigs with fencing, you can expect a costly endeavor. A fence of heavy gauge wire would be necessary, fastened with strong, secure brace poles four to five feet apart. Pigs will easily destroy wire fencing when food is just on the other side. It would seem that electric fencing would be economically more practical. However, my research has not uncovered any sure methods of excluding wild pigs with the use of electric fencing. Again, the peanut butter method as described under deer, elk and moose would probably increase the chances of an electric fence working.

Most states that suffer major damages caused by wild pigs rely on live or cage traps to eliminate the problem animals. Great Smoky Mountains National Park officials have often used traps to remove wild pigs.

Chapter 7

Rodents and Other Mammals

This chapter will provide valuable information about selected rodents and other species of mammals that often become a nuisance. Actually, there are thousands of rodents and small mammals in North America, but some are far more destructive than others. These animals vary considerably in size, but size has little to do with the damages they can inflict.

Rodents have four incisors — two on the top and two on the bottom. Most rodents rely on these incisors for survival. You could say that teeth of each rodent have a significant purpose.

There are mammals other than rodents that I have included in this section. Rabbits and opossums are two such critters, both of which have caused their share of problems for man.

Beavers

There is probably no harder worker in North America than the beaver. The expression "busy as a beaver" is a very meaningful and powerful suggestion. In fact, these workaholics cause more problems in some states and provinces than all other mammals combined. Prior to 1990, when the Minnesota Division of

Enforcement assisted in the removal of beavers and dams, conservation officers spent 15,000 hours each year, at a cost of $100,000, to control nuisance beavers.

The beaver inhabits portions of every state and province. The only places you will not find these rodents are coastlines and deserts. The beaver is also responsible for the arrival of early settlers in some regions. In the early 1700s, beaver fur was sought by trappers. This often led to the development of settlements. Some regions saw declines of beavers when the value of the pelts soared, but that soon changed. Today, North America's largest rodent, and the only one to have a broad, flattened tail, thrives most everywhere.

The beaver's natural habitat consists of low, marshy areas. However, they can survive anywhere water is available. That includes the high elevations of the Rocky Mountains. These aquatic animals maneuver slowly on land, but they are perfectionists when it comes to swimming.

An adult beaver could easily surpass three feet in length and weigh up to 50 pounds. I have heard of some beavers that weighed more than 80 pounds. The beaver's fur is waterproof and very course, designed to keep them as warm as necessary. The beaver's feet are unique in that the smaller front feet can carry and dig while the larger, fully webbed back feet allow them to swim (Figure 7-1). They have five toes and strong claws on each foot.

Beavers give birth to their litters in late spring and early summer. A female may have up to eight youngsters, but family colonies are typical. A colony usually consists of both parents (beavers mate for life) and kits, together with offspring from the previous two breeding seasons.

When it comes to eating, beavers rely solely on vegetation. The bark and twigs of such trees as alder, aspen, birch, maple and willow satisfy their needs most of the time. However, in the summer months they eat many small woody plants, water lilies, cattails and grasses. During the winter, they benefit the most from

Figure 7-1. The beaver uses the webbed hind feet for swimming and the front feet for digging.

their sharp incisors. They may fell trees as large as your thigh, and transport them to their lodge. But beavers also feed on some crops such as corn.

Identifying beaver sign is not really difficult. Their webbed tracks are one indication of their existence in a given area. However, flooding is usually an obvious sign that is unmistakable. You may also spot beaver dams and lodges.

Beavers use a variety of items to build their lodges. It usually appears as a heap of sticks and debris plastered together with mud. Each lodge consists of a doorway and a ledge above the water where they spend much of their time.

Beaver trails are very common near water. You will also see gnawed and felled trees if a beaver has set up home nearby. You will seldom see beaver scat though, since they usually defecate under the water. Another common sight is beaver slides. These slicks can be spotted along banks or hills surrounding water.

Scent mounds are often detected visually, or by smell. The scent mound consists of a pile of grass, mud or other debris about

Table 18. Beaver damage categories in descending order of significance, as reported by 43 states. Source: Survey compiled by Minnesota Department of Natural Resources in cooperation with the Minnesota Department of Agriculture.

State	Damage #1	Damage #2	Damage #3
AK	Flooded roads	Gnawing	Trout stream
AL	Gnawing	Flooded timber	Flooded fields
AR	Flooded timber	Flooded fields	Flooded roads
AZ	Irrigation system	Gnawing	
CO	Irrigation system	Flooded roads	Gnawing
CT	Flooded roads	Flooded homes	Flooded fields
DE	Flooded roads	Flooded fields	Flooded timber
FL	Flooded roads	Flooded timber	Gnawing
GA	Flooded timber	Flooded roads	Flooded fields
IA	Flooded fields	Flooded roads	Flooded timber
ID	Flooded roads	Flooded fields	
IL	Flooded fields	Flooded roads	Gnawing
KS	Flooded fields	Gnawing	Flooded roads
KY	Flooded fields	Flooded timber	Flooded roads
LA	Flooded timber	Flooded roads	Flooded fields
MA	Flooded roads	Flooded timber	Flooded wells
MD	Flooded roads	Flooded timber	Gnawing
ME	Flooded roads	Gnawing	Flooded fields
MI	Flooded roads	Flooded timber	Flooded fields
MN	Flooded roads	Flooded fields	Flooded timber
MO	Flooded fields	Flooded roads	Gnawing
MS	Flooded timber	Flooded roads	Flooded fields
MT	Flooded fields	Flooded roads	Gnawing
NC	Flooded timber	Flooded roads	Gnawing
NE	Flooded fields	Flooded roads	Gnawing
NH	Flooded homes	Gnawing	Flooded roads
NJ	Flooded roads	Gnawing	Flooded homes
NM	Flooded fields	Gnawing	
NV	Irrigation system	Gnawing	Flooded roads
NY	Flooded roads	Flooded fields	Flooded timber
OH	Flooded fields	Flooded roads	Gnawing
OR	Flooded fields	Irrigation system	Gnawing
PA	Flooded fields	Flooded roads	Gnawing
RI	Flooded roads	Flooded timber	Gnawing
SC	Flooded timber	Flooded roads	Flooded fields
TN	Flooded timber	Flooded fields	Gnawing
TX	Flooded timber	Flooded roads	Gnawing
UT	Flooded roads	Gnawing	Flooded fields
VA	Gnawing	Flooded roads	Flooded timber
WI	Flooded roads	Trout stream	Flooded timber
WV	Flooded timber	Flooded fields	Flooded roads
WY	Flooded fields	Irrigation system	Gnawing

This large tree was felled by a beaver. Notice the center of the stump that remains where the tree once stood. A beaver fells a tree by working in an even circle around the trunk.

one foot tall. The mound actually has a sweet stench (it has been used in perfume), an aroma from the beaver's castor gland located at the base of their tail.

So, do beavers cause many problems for people? To say the least, flooding (caused by beaver dams) damage alone results in many other types of problems. Flooding can devastate crops, kill valuable plant life, cause erosion, destroy timber, and seriously damage roads or create hazardous driving conditions for motorists.

A survey conducted by the Minnesota Department of Natural Resources showed various types of beaver damage complaints as reported by 43 states. The survey asked each state to list five types of beaver damage complaints in order of importance. I have included the first three types in Table 18. The survey also reported that all states provide technical assistance to agencies and landowners having beaver problems. At least 66 percent provide direct removal of beavers and 50 percent provide removal of beaver dams by agency personnel. Nearly half of the states issue beaver and/or dam removal permits, and 44 percent allow property owners to remove nuisance beavers without a permit. Open trapping seasons are allowed in all states, while 21 percent allow hunting of beavers.

Before taking it upon yourself to remove a beaver's dam, or trap or kill a beaver, check the regulations in the state or province where you reside (you may need a designated permit). To hunt beavers successfully, you will want to look for them in the early morning and late evening hours. Beavers rest during the day and are primarily active at night.

Tearing holes in a beaver dam will seldom discourage a beaver. Usually, within 24 to 48 hours the beaver will patch the hole. However, totally removing dams and/or lodges may prove effective in discouraging beavers. It is vitally important, though, to remove every portion of the structure. This can be done with heavy equipment, or perhaps by hand if you have the time and a solid back.

Scarecrows, noisemakers and powerful lighting devices will not discourage nuisance beavers. However, an experienced beaver trapper can reduce or eliminate a beaver population from any site. As discussed previously in this book, many trappers will jump at the chance to do nuisance animal work, particularly when pelt prices are high. Live trapping is very difficult and seldom effective. Both leg-hold and Conibear traps will work, though many trappers prefer the Conibear.

Because the beaver is large and powerful, a skilled trapper is often a better choice than doing it yourself. However, if you want to attempt this without help, I will pass along a few suggestions. Many veteran trappers use these techniques.

You must place your trap in the proper location if it is to work effectively. Preferred locations for steel leg-hold traps are where beavers leave the water and by their dams. A scent mound also provides a good location to set your trap. A commercially produced lure, available from trapping supply companies, will serve as an attractant.

The leg-hold trap should be placed about three to six inches below the water. If placed near a beaver slide, it will help to set the trap about three inches off to the side. This prevents them from centering the trap. Some trappers rely on a weight to drown beaver, but a wire through a one way slide, fastened to the trap chain and a heavy anchor, also works. You should stake one end of the wire beneath the trap and tie the other end to the anchor in deep water.

The 330 sized Conibear trap kills quickly and seldom allows escapes. This trap also works well partially above or totally below the surface in shallow or deep water. You should place the trap at a beaver hole, in runways between bank dens, lodges and feeding areas, or at crossings on top of dams or directly below dams. Conibear traps should be secured with stakes and wired to the bank. Action may come quicker if you block off paths around your trap. An arrangement of debris will cause the beaver to travel through the trap opening. You can also tear a hole in the beaver dam and set your trap immediately to prompt action. Beavers easily hear the sounds of running water and will often come to inspect the damage quickly.

One low cost way of controlling flood water caused by beaver dams is to install drain pipes. One or two eight-foot lengths of PVC (six-inch or larger diameter recommended) pipe can be placed in the dam to keep the water at a desired level. Two pipes are usually necessary for larger waterways. By using eight-foot lengths, you can allow the pipes to overhang by two and a half or three feet on each end of the dam. This stops the beaver from plugging the ends of the pipe. You should still check the pipes periodically and clean them when necessary.

If you have beavers near your home and want to protect shrubs and trees, you can keep them from gnawing on them by placing a heavy, securely fastened, woven wire fence around them. The fence should be at least 40 inches tall.

After all this, it's time I said something positive about beavers.

They often create habitat and ponds that provide many species of wildlife with more suitable homes. These creations may also increase hunting, fishing and wildlife and scenic viewing opportunities. Their impounded water may also furnish moisture to adjacent agricultural lands during dry periods. Farmers may also use beaver ponds to irrigate livestock. Before taking action against a beaver colony, a landowner should first consider the beneficial aspects.

Muskrats

There are few places the muskrat does not inhabit. This rat-like creature is found in every region of North America except the dryer regions in Arizona and California. The muskrat prefers wetland habit, thriving in both fresh and saltwater marshes. Any slow-moving or still water lake, pond, swamp or ditch could become a home for this mammal. Despite the loss of wetland areas in the U.S., it continues to flourish.

The muskrat earned its name from the musk glands found near the base of its tail. Like other rodents, the muskrat has a pair of sharp incisors on the upper and lower jaws that can promptly chew through thick vegetation. They commonly use aquatic vegetation to build their dome huts. Muskrat huts are similar to the houses built by beavers, except smaller. These houses extend above the water level about two feet or more, but they have several doors under the water. Many have claimed the muskrat can survive under water for about 30 minutes.

Muskrats also use dens for their homes. You will seldom notice these homes, however, because the openings to them are under the water near dams or banks. To find them, look closely just under the water as you patiently walk dams or banks. You may also see trails near the water's edge that lead directly to the dens. Muskrat burrowing can often lead to severe damage to pond and lake dams.

Most of the muskrat's diet consists of various types of aquatic vegetation, cattails, grasses and water lilies. Occasionally, they will also feed upon clams, mussels and crayfish. Observant individuals may find remnants of mussels or crayfish along banks or dams. When crop fields such as corn, soybeans and wheat are located close to water, the muskrat will look to them for food.

An adult muskrat will usually measure 20 to 25 inches from the head to the start of the tail. The skinny tail, characteristic of the muskrat, is about 10 inches long. The muskrat has a reddish brown body, gray belly and black tail. You can often see them at a distance because they have a very glossy hide. However, when the muskrat swims, you can only see their head sticking above the water surface. The hind foot is about two and a half to three inches long, while the front foot seldom exceeds one to one a half inches in length. The front and back feet have five toes (Figure 7-2).

You may also find scat if muskrats are plentiful in a given area. Unlike the beaver, which usually defecates under the water, muskrats commonly defecate on logs or rocks in the water. This is because they often spend hours resting on logs and rocks barely above the water surface.

Few crops are lost due to muskrats feeding on them, but

Figure 7-2. Muskrat tracks resemble the tracks of beavers. However, the muskrat does not have webbed hind feet.

occasionally the burrowing of these rodents will cause flooding into crop fields. More damaging, though, is the loss of a water resource due to their burrowing. Burrowing can result in a weak, leaking dam. Their dens can also cause injuries to livestock that visit the water source. For these reasons, you should close dens with rocks and dirt immediately. Some landowners will line the banks/dams of their valued ponds and lakes with rip-rap to prevent further damage.

Due to the muskrat's breeding practices, they can overpopulate in a given area rather quickly. Muskrats may have four to six litters per year, with up to 10 youngsters in each litter. This often creates a problem for a landowner when they attempt to remove nuisance muskrats.

If an area becomes infested with muskrats, the only solution might be removing the problem animals. However, before killing or trapping muskrats, check the regulations in the state or province where the problem has occurred. The muskrat is considered a furbearing animal and each state/province has regulations applying to the harvest of this animal.

Before trapping muskrats, you must know that they still inhabit the area. Muskrats will stay in a given area, but only if food is plentiful. Fresh tracks and/or traces of food they have eaten should be nearby.

Many trappers use a size 110 Conibear trap to take muskrats. These traps can be set directly in the middle of a trail the muskrat uses along a bank, or at a den entrance. Traps set on trails work best when you place them about two or three inches into the water, or just barely under the surface. It will help to pile debris around the sides of the trail so the muskrat must pass through the trap. When setting the trap at a den entrance, you must also put it where the muskrat has to pass through when it leaves. A heavy vertical stake is necessary to secure the traps.

You can also consider constructing a physical structure to prevent muskrat burrowing. Place sand or pea gravel on the front side of the dam, one to two feet under the water and about two to three feet above the water surface. Muskrats, after attempting to dig in the sand or pea gravel, will usually decide to burrow elsewhere.

You can also reduce muskrat damage by removing the aquatic growth they feed upon. Once a food supply expires, they will move. If removal is necessary, I would suggest you begin in the winter months. Muskrats often stay in a given area throughout the winter months.

Opossums

I saw my first opossum about 30 years ago. It was a female with 10 or more youngsters fastened to her fur. Female opossums often give birth to 15 or more helpless youngsters. At birth, they will crawl into the female's pouch for warmth and food. Several weeks later, the youngsters leave the pouch and cling to their mother's fur as she travels.

The opossum is the only animal in North America that has a pouch. It is also believed that the opossum has managed to survive for more than 60 million years. Today, the opossum inhabits all of the Midwestern states eastward to the Atlantic Ocean as far north as Maine. Opossums are also found near the Pacific coast, but they are not present in the Rocky Mountains.

An adult male opossum can have a body length of two feet and weigh up to seven pounds. Females seldom weigh more than four pounds. Each has 12 inches of tail which comes in handy for wrapping around the limb of a tree and hanging upside down. The ears and the skinny tail of the opossum are hairless. Their body fur is light gray but the dense belly fur is white. It normally moves slowly and will sometimes play "possum" when threatened. When playing possum, it curls up and lies in a motionless state. However, it is not unusual for this mammal to "hiss" when threatened. Though they are nocturnal, you can sometimes spot them at dawn and dusk.

The opossum is often found around woods and fields near

water. It prefers to den under roots or stumps, or in hollow trees and logs. It is a strong survivor because it eats almost anything. True, they do scavenge and clean up the woods of dead animals. But they also eat acorns, persimmons, insects and earthworms. They occasionally feed on birds, mice, shrews and moles. Surprisingly, they will also eat eggs from the ground nests of many birds, and they can become notorious killers of poultry when opportunity allows. When garbage or pet foods are available, they will not hesitate to take advantage of a free handout.

Many trappers claim that male opossums kill more poultry than do females. However, this may be due to the male's larger size. When they stalk their victims, they like to surprise them. The opossum does not move swiftly. They must rely on sneaking up on their prey. Opossums that have found an easy food source near a residence will often den in nearby hollow trees, in barns, or under poultry houses.

The opossum has five toes on each "handlike" foot (Figure 7-3). Their toes are widespread and they have a clawless thumb. The tracks are about an inch and a half long. In sand or snow, you may also see drag marks from the tail.

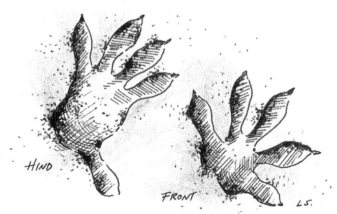

Figure 7-3. The hind feet of the opossum are slightly longer than the handlike front feet. The hind feet also have "thumbs" that are separated from the other toes.

Most states do not have closed seasons on opossums. However, before removing a nuisance opossum, check the game laws in the state or province where the problem occurs.

Nuisance opossums are not difficult to trap. Live traps (No. 3 or 3A) and double coil spring traps (No. 2) work best. Several bait items will attract problem opossums. Meat scraps, fish and fruits will attract them. You may also consider placing a shiny item at the trap site since the opossum has a very curious nature. If a problem occurs around buildings, place the trap wherever the opossum enters.

Cubby traps will also remove problem opossums. The cubby set is a three-sided house about two feet long made of small logs or rocks about one foot high. A handy hollow log will make a good cubby. You can cover the top of the house with branches. You should hide the trap with limbs and debris, except for the open end, and place bait near the rear of the cubby. A leg-hold trap placed about a half inch below ground level should be set in front of the bait.

You should handle any live-trapped opossum with care. They will readily use their claws when threatened. The opossum also has an anal gland that omits a very undesirable odor.

You can prevent poultry losses caused by opossums by placing an electric wire at the top of an existing fence. Poultry and field fencing alone will not keep opossums out, since they are good climbers. They can be kept from getting into garbage cans by placing a stretch cord over the lid and fastening it from one handle to the other.

Opossums, where their numbers have increased, often cause problems for landowners. However, they seldom become a nuisance animal except during winter months when food availability decreases.

Prairie Dogs

At one time, landowners considered the prairie dog a major

nuisance. Because of their burrowing, they were often slaughtered. Some individuals even poisoned entire colonies of prairie dogs. Today, however, we have come to realize that they help the environment in which they live. More about that in a moment.

The prairie dog is actually a rodent. They earned the title "dog" because of their ability to yip loudly. They inhabit the Rocky Mountain and plain regions, particularly the grasslands and foothills from the southernmost boundaries of Texas as far north as the Canadian border.

Prairie dogs do not move from one region to another. Instead, they stay in one general area to make their own "town." It is not uncommon for several hundred prairie dogs to exist in one town within a couple of acres. Many years ago, some prairie dog towns consisted of thousands of the rodents. Each prairie dog town is made up of numerous burrows. These dome-like burrows may extend several feet into the ground and connect with a tunnel. The mounds above the burrows, however, come in handy when the prairie dog needs to scan the area. If they spot danger (their eyesight is their best sense), they will promptly drop back into the burrow.

Prairie dogs are highly social, preferring to live in colonies and create towns.

Prairie dogs eat

many varieties of vegetation. The area surrounding their burrows is usually devoid of vegetation because they will feed on grasses when they emerge from the den. They will also feed on sagebrush and some insects. They feed during the daylight hours but may stay underground during the hottest part of the day.

The young are born in the spring. A female prairie dog will usually give birth to six to 10 pups. After a few weeks, the young leave the underground to follow their mother when she feeds. However, they quickly learn to watch for predators. Though many ground carnivores love to eat prairie dogs, this rodent must also endure attacks from the sky. Eagles and hawks commonly prey upon unsuspecting prairie dogs.

Although prairie dogs do compete with livestock because they eat the same vegetation, it is still not fully understood if this affects livestock production. The size of a prairie dog town may have much to do with how much livestock will suffer. However, numerous burrows do cause significant erosion on slopes. Their burrows are also dangerous to the health of grazing livestock. It has also been noted that prairie dog burrows attract rattlesnakes during the heat of the day.

You may harvest prairie dogs in most states at any time but you may need a hunting license before taking action against those that have become a nuisance. Check with your local game and fish department before hunting. It is also important that you do not mistake a prairie dog for a black-footed ferret. The black-footed ferret is an endangered species that often resides in prairie dog towns.

Barriers can be placed around burrows to discourage prairie dogs. In fact, hay bales that surround their burrow will limit their view. Some landowners have also burned prairie grasses, while others have plowed prairie dog towns.

Trapping is slow in removing prairie dogs since they must be dealt with one-on-one. The Conibear No. 110 body-grip trap may work best. They should be placed at the base of the mound by the burrow. However, shooting problem prairie dogs is often more practicable. The hunter must remain hidden at a distance. The .22-250 is often used but the smaller caliber .22 will be sufficient if you can stay within 40 to 80 yards of the burrows.

In heavily populated prairie dog areas where they have caused major problems, gas cartridges can be considered. Gas cartridges, when burning and placed into a burrow, will put off poisonous gases that will travel through prairie dog chambers. Before using gas cartridges, contact your game and fish department or the USDA/APHIS/ADC office.

It should be understood that prairie dogs are a valuable resource for many reasons. First, consider that their burrows create homes and refuges for many animals. Many predators rely on prairie dogs for their next meal. Some plants also flourish in the rich, aerated soil common in many prairie dog towns. These plants provide nourishing food for many animals.

Rabbits

According to a report published by the National Agricultural Statistics Service, surveys of U.S. farms indicated that rabbits and rodents ranked second in the category of animals that caused damage from 1988 through 1989. More than 26 percent of the farms that reported damages caused by animals put the blame on rabbits and rodents. The areas of the Northeast and North Central reported the highest percentage of damages.

The cottontail rabbit is the most common species of rabbits and hares. Other members of the rabbit and hare family include the jackrabbit, European rabbit and varying (snowshoe) hare. However, this section will focus on the widespread cottontail rabbit. Cottontails are found in almost every state in the U.S. and in the southernmost regions of some provinces in Canada.

Rabbits are seldom mistaken for any other mammal. These small animals get their name from their round, fluffy cotton-like tail. The cottontail's fur ranges from reddish brown to gray, which it sheds twice each year.

Cottontail rabbits live in a variety of habitats. There are brush cottontails, and close relatives such as the larger swamp rabbit and desert cottontail. Most of the common Eastern cottontails, however, require dense vegetation for survival. Bramble bushes, thick honeysuckle and log jams provide the necessary cover for cottontails. It will occasionally use ground burrows of other animals to escape from predators.

Perhaps you have heard the expression "breed like a rabbit." This comes from the female rabbit's ability to give birth to several litters from early spring to late summer. Most litters consist of four to six youngsters. However, studies have indicated that in some geographical areas up to 80 percent of the young rabbits die before reaching six months of age. Cold temperatures, predators and, in some areas, loss of habitat are to blame for their deaths.

When preparing for birth, the female cottontail pulls out her fur and places it in the nest. The youngsters need this fur since they are born naked. They weigh one ounce or less and will stay in the nests for about two to three weeks. By this time the mother rabbit has been bred again and must think about the upcoming litter.

The rabbit eats a variety of plant life, but it does not favor fescue grass. They feed upon several woody plants, sumac (a common winter food), clover, honeysuckle and many others.

Many orchards suffer economic losses because of damages caused by rabbits. Rabbits also eat flowers and many vegetables grown in gardens. Of the vegetables, rabbits seem to prefer beans, cabbage, carrot tops, lettuce and peas. Damages to plants such as corn, cucumbers and squash, however, should not be blamed on rabbits. Young trees and evergreens are also favorite foods.

The species causing damage to flower and vegetable gardens can sometimes be known by the way the plant is bitten. The woodchuck usually bites off a plant evenly. However, the rabbit will strip the bark off of young trees only a short distance above the

The cottontail rabbit often causes damage to flower and vegetable gardens, evergreens and various trees.

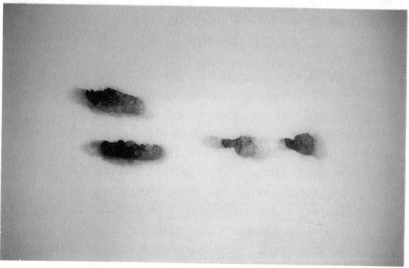

The track set of a rabbit is about twelve inches long. It places the longer hind feet ahead of the shorter front feet when it hops and runs.

148

ground. This may also kill the tree. This damage should be examined closely, though, since the meadow mouse also feeds on the bark of young trees. The rabbits' teeth are larger, and bite marks on the tree differs from the smaller teeth marks of the mouse. Droppings may also be found where rabbits feed consistently. Droppings are usually tan to brown, about one-fourth inch each and round. One clump of droppings may consist of 12 or more pellets.

Because the cottontail rabbit is so widespread, damages are not limited to rural areas. People in major metropolitan areas also experience rabbit problems. My in-laws live in a suburb of Chicago but often complain of rabbits eating their flowers.

Rabbits can be identified by their tracks if you are fortunate enough to find them in loose soil or snow. They have five toes on the front feet and four toes on the hind feet. It is difficult to see the toe prints, however, since they are covered with fur. The length of a running cottontail track set (includes all four feet) measures about one foot in length. The hopping or running rabbit commonly places its hind feet in front of the front feet. However, rabbit tracks also resemble squirrel tracks. The primary difference is in the overall length of the track set. The track set of the squirrel is only about six to eight inches long.

Fencing will protect gardens and trees from rabbits, but this method of protection can lead to great expense. Poultry fencing is recommended, but you should anchor it tightly and bury it two to three inches under the ground to prevent rabbits from going under the guard. Hardware cloth can also be used to prevent rabbit damage to trees. The cloth should be at least two to three feet tall. Rabbits are small animals, but they will stand on their hind feet to reach food.

A Federal prison in North Carolina had their escape alarms tripped more than 100 times when cottontail rabbits activated infrared sensors on the security fences. ADC installed a polytape electric fencing system to exclude the rabbits and loaned live traps to prison officials to capture rabbits that made their way into the facility. For more information about polytape fencing, see "Deer" in the chapter titled "Hoofed Mammals."

To discourage rabbits, you might consider using a repellent that contains "thiram." Some repellents with thiram can be used directly while others must be diluted with water. You can spray or brush on the repellent. Before using any repellent, read the label carefully. Plants meant for human consumption should not be treated. You can purchase rabbit repellents from many nurseries, feed and hardware stores.

Reducing preferred habitat is another way to control rabbit populations. However, I would suggest you consider other alternatives unless this becomes absolutely necessary to reduce damage. In many areas, particularly those with few grown up fence rows where extensive farming has destroyed dense vegetation that rabbits need, habitat is necessary for the cottontail to survive. Destroying this habitat also removes habitat that many other mammals need. If removal becomes necessary, though, you should take out log jams, thick brush and stumps. The closer your gardens, trees and shrubs are located to rabbit habitat, the better the chance that damage will occur.

Trapping and hunting may effectively control rabbit populations. However, rabbits are game animals in most states and protected except during special trapping and hunting seasons. Exceptions may be made to landowners that suffer extensive damages. Check game regulations in the state or province where you live before taking action.

When using live traps, I would suggest the No. 2 wire type. You should place the trap close to thick areas or at locations where damage occurs. Sliced apples, some green vegetables, corn from the cob, and of course carrots, work well as bait. When transporting trapped rabbits, you should let them loose in areas where preferred habitat exists.

Many garden shops sell realistic replicas of hawks and owls. Hawks and owls are natural predators of rabbits. When these decoys are placed near gardens and trees where damage occurs (I would recommend using two or three), they may keep rabbits away. Scarecrows, however, are not highly effective tools for discouraging nuisance rabbits.

On the positive side of rabbits, you could say they are often welcome sights to our landscape. I have suffered damages caused by rabbits, especially to my vegetable garden, but still enjoy their presence. I often make it a point to look out my window in the early morning and late evening hours just to watch these primarily nocturnal mammals going about their business.

Squirrels

If you read the introduction to this book, you may remember that the gray squirrel was the first species mentioned. Squirrels have provided me with plenty of pleasure, as I have always enjoyed their company. However, squirrels also cause substantial problems for many landowners, including myself.

Of the many states and provinces that my research led me to, at least one claimed that people complained more about squirrels than any other species. A biologist from Louisiana said the state issues the most Nuisance Animal Control permits to individuals complaining about problem squirrels. A summary report showed that 105 permits were issued in 1995 to remove nuisance animals such as armadillos, beavers, coyotes, raccoons and rabbits. The state found it necessary to issue more than half of the permits, though, for nuisance squirrels.

There are several species of squirrels in North America. Some are of the tree dwelling family and some of the ground family. At least two can glide through the air with the greatest of ease. They are known as the northern and southern flying squirrels.

Of the tree dwelling types, the gray and red fox squirrel are the most common. The gray squirrel inhabits most of the Eastern U.S. and portions of some states in the far West. The red fox squirrel is restricted to the Eastern half of the U.S. In the forest regions of the Rocky Mountains of the U.S. and Canada, as well as the lower elevation woodland areas of many northern states and provinces, you will encounter the red squirrel (the king of all chattering animals in my opinion). Flying squirrels inhabit the entire eastern U.S. and many provinces of Canada as far north as Alaska.

All squirrels are hard workers. They will do their best to store food in the fall months to prepare for the winter. Some will work all day, burying and hiding nuts and pine cones. Unfortunately, even though their sense of smell is fair, they find only a small percentage of what they hide. They must also compete for the same foods that many other animals prefer.

Tree squirrels have one or two litters each year. One litter arrives in the spring and the other in midsummer. Litter numbers usually consist of two to seven. The youngsters have no hair at birth and weigh less than one ounce.

The red fox squirrel is the largest of the squirrel family. There is only a little difference in the size of gray and northern red squirrels. The northern flying squirrel is the smallest. However, all members of the squirrel family prefer to den in trees. The gray and red fox squirrel often builds nests of twigs and leaves, as well as using holes in trees to spend their nights. Red squirrels also den in trees, but occasionally they will hole up in the ground. Of the tree dwelling squirrels, only the flying squirrel is active at night. Flying squirrels actually glide after spreading their skin and using their tail as a rudder.

Squirrels are prolific eaters of nuts. They also eat a variety of fruits, berries and buds. The red squirrels of the far north and west also eat the seeds of Ponderosa and white pine cones. Even the gray and red fox squirrel will not hesitate to eat pine cones when poor nut masts occur. Squirrels also eat corn (both the hybrid and sweet types) and bird eggs. Occasionally, squirrels will raid bird feeders.

It is not always the squirrel's preferred foods that cause problems. However, for some landowners, such as myself, their desire for hickory nuts has created serious problems. A large hickory tree that stands next to my deck at the back of the house produces a bumper crop of nuts each year. Without fail, the squirrels begin dining on the nuts every August. They continue feeding on the hickory nuts through September, their hulls and cuttings dropping to the deck daily. These nut droppings also clog the gutters and damage the roof. Squirrels also inflict serious damage to trees, including the pecan crops in the southern states.

Squirrels can also short power lines as they chew on them or walk on them to get from one location to another. Many people in residential areas complain about squirrels because they build nests in attics, chimneys, garages and other outbuildings, as well as weaken gutters as they use them to scamper back and forth. Squirrels may also enter dwellings to hide food or build nests. On two occasions, before closing off the fireplace chimney with wire, I had squirrels get into the house. I don't know if you have ever tried to catch a wild gray squirrel with a dip net, but I can tell you first hand that this is a very tricky, frustrating experience.

Problem squirrels are often heard on the roofs of houses, particularly when overhanging tree limbs are present. You may also find the hulls of nuts where they feed, or signs of leaf nests. Gray and red fox squirrels are occasionally heard barking. Red squirrels frequently chatter at anything that moves and some things that do not move.

Squirrel tracks are similar to those made by rabbits, but the track set of a squirrel is usually shorter. The gray and red fox squirrel have five toes on each foot. However, one toe on each front foot is shorter than the others. When it moves about on the ground, the feet are usually paired.

In cornfields, squirrels often climb up the stalks to get to the corn. However, they seldom break the stalks as do raccoons. These rodents will usually break off the cobs and carry them to another location to begin eating. Cob remnants, or a few yellow kernels found at one location, are a good indication that a squirrel caused

At least one state reported that they receive more complaints about squirrels than any other animal.

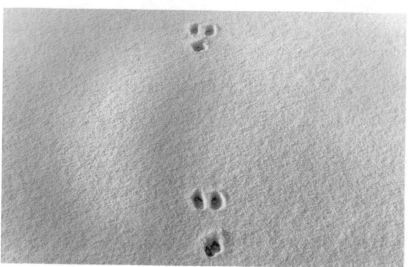

Squirrel tracks resemble rabbit tracks. However, notice how the front and hind feet of the squirrel are paired.

the damage.

To discourage squirrels from visiting trees, you should remove as many branches as possible on all surrounding trees. A few feet of air between limbs will not keep a squirrel from jumping from one limb to another. You can also consider putting aluminum duct pipe around the bottom of the tree. The higher up you go, the better, but be sure to use a piece large enough to allow for tree growth. Squirrels are at a great disadvantage when they try to climb up a slick surface.

Bird feeders can be protected by placing the feeder on a tall pole and placing an umbrella like piece of metal (about 15 inches in diameter) at the top of the pole just under the feeder. When a squirrel climbs the pole, it will be unable to get to the feeder.

To keep squirrels from entering chimneys and gutters, cover the openings with a tightly woven mesh wire fence. Flying squirrels are very small and can squeeze through a two-inch opening. Attic openings should also be closed.

Mothballs may effectively keep squirrels away, but this prevention method is often temporary. Place an abundance of mothballs in areas where problems occur. House cats may also help keep squirrels away, but cats roaming freely may kill songbirds and other animals.

Before killing and trapping nuisance squirrels, check the regulations in the state or province where the problem occurred. Many squirrels are considered game animals and can be taken only during limited seasons. Others may be fully protected.

A No. 2 live trap is effective when baited with apple slices, corn from the cob, nuts, peanut butter and sunflower seeds. You should place traps at the base of trees. Before relocating a trapped squirrel, talk with a wildlife official.

If the wildlife agency in your area allows, you can consider using a rat trap to catch small problem squirrels. You may also want to shoot them with a .22 rifle. Care must be used when shooting a .22 rifle, though, since these small bullets can travel for long distances.

Although I encounter nuisance squirrels around my home, I still enjoy their presence. In fact, I have placed feeders of corn nearby to photograph them. Squirrels are also good for the environment, since they disperse seeds into the ground and enhance future growth of many plants and trees.

Woodchucks

Traditionally called groundhogs, woodchucks are actually rodents and members of the squirrel family. To some degree, you could say they are over-sized ground squirrels. Woodchucks do not "chuck wood," however, they can climb trees. Occasionally, I have seen these nervous critters scramble up a tree and rest on a limb so that they could inspect the surrounding area for predators.

Although the woodchuck is diurnal, it spends many hours underground each day in the safety of its tunnels and burrows. These hefty, powerful rodents may reach a length of 25 inches or more and weigh up to 10 pounds. They inhabit every state east of the Dakotas except Florida. Woodchucks live in nearly every province of Canada and Alaska. Their close cousin, the marmot, survives in the high country of the Western U.S. and within the boundaries of some western provinces of Canada.

The woodchuck is an extraordinary excavator that often digs its burrows along banks and hillsides. However, when only level ground is available, they will not hesitate to dig out a new home close to a food source. Most tunnels extend about four feet into the ground and connect with a chamber where the woodchuck spends its time resting during the heat of the day. The excavating process does not take long if the groundhog can work with loose soil. In fact, they can completely build a tunnel and chamber within a few hours.

The groundhog is not a sociable animal. Each den usually contains only one woodchuck. Several burrows in a small area do not mean that one rodent resides in each. On the contrary, one groundhog may have more than one entrance to his chamber. He also has escape tunnels in areas where he feeds.

To say the least, the woodchuck is a neurotic animal. I have often wondered if their little hearts pound rapidly each time they leave their burrows, because they constantly stay on the lookout for danger. Each time they decide to eat, they will rise slightly out of their burrow and look around for dangers. This procedure can last for 30 minutes. During this process, they never move any part of their body except the head. Once all is clear, they will begin feeding close to the burrow. Even then, though, they will only eat for a minute or two before standing up on their back legs to view their surroundings. Apparently, they do handle this nervousness well. Groundhogs often live to five years of age.

Woodchucks are true hibernators. In the late fall and early winter months they go into a deep sleep and do not arouse again until February or March. Breeding, however, usually begins immediately. One month later, the female will give birth to four or five hairless and blind youngsters.

The woodchuck is primarily a vegetarian but it occasionally eats insects. It does not move long distances to find food. It may move a few hundred yards to get to an agricultural field, but it does not leave a home range. Woodchucks will feed on whatever browse is available close to its burrow.

Groundhogs eat various types of foliage, and they dearly love alfalfa, carrot tops, clover, corn, fruits and soybeans. Farmers often despise the presence of woodchucks because of their ability to consume large quantities of soybeans. Vegetable gardens are also attractive to woodchucks. They will not pass up some bean plants, cantaloupe, lettuce, peas and tomatoes. Nurseries also dread the presence of groundhogs because they will eat the bark of some trees. It has been said that the woodchuck requires about one pound of forage per day.

When groundhogs feed on plants, they will cleanly bite off the stems. Deer often rip or tear the stems of plants, while rabbits

The woodchuck eats about one pound of forage daily. This forage may consist of woody plants and grasses, or a few of the vegetables in your garden.

may strip the bark. You can tell the difference in the feeding patterns of the these animals when you examine the damage closely. Deer are also browsers and will skip around here and there in crop fields and large gardens. Woodchucks tend to feed in a given area. I have inspected many soybean fields damaged by groundhogs. They will often bite off the stem of every bean plant within a 50-yard radius of their burrow.

You may notice the presence of a woodchuck if you hear a sharp "whistle." These rodents commonly whistle when alarmed by predators and man. By the time you hear this, though, the groundhog is usually heading straight for its burrow.

Tracks of groundhogs differ from those of other species that feed in crop fields and gardens. They have five toes on each foot. However, you will seldom see the thumb on the somewhat shorter front feet (Figure 7-4).

The burrows of woodchucks create hazards for livestock since they may step in them. Burrows and tunnels also weaken foundations of buildings. Groundhogs often select barns or other outbuildings away from people for their dens.

In most areas, the woodchuck is considered a varmint. Thus, they can be hunted or trapped at any time. However, before hunting, check the regulations in the state or province where the damage occurs.

Gas cartridges are often placed deep in burrows for relief of

Figure 7-4. Although the woodchuck has five toes on each foot, you will not usually see the thumb print in the tracks of the front feet.

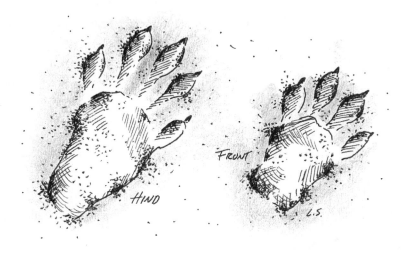

problem groundhogs. A fuse is lit and the cartridge ignites. Rock or dirt should then be placed over the entrance of the den, or other holes nearby. However, please note that any other animal that happens to be in the burrow may also suffer the consequences of a gas cartridge. Gas cartridges are available at most feed stores and some hardware outlets.

Effective hunting will also reduce populations of problem woodchucks. The .22-250 caliber rifle is often favored, but the .22 also works well if you can set up close to the burrows and use a telescopic sight. You will usually find the main burrow in dense vegetation along the edges of fields or gardens. Holes found in the feeding area are probably just an escape tunnel. Defined trails leading from the burrow to the feeding area are easily identified. The rodents are most active in the early morning and late afternoon on hot summer days.

The 220 Conibear trap placed near the entrance of the den works effectively but should not be used if pets freely roam the area. On slopes, you will want to place the trap over the hole and stake it from above.

To protect a garden from woodchucks, you might consider a three-foot tall fence with only one by two-inch openings. You should also bury the fence at least six inches under the ground. Finally, brace the fence securely with strong posts. A single wire electric fence, placed about six inches off the ground and a few inches outside the previously mentioned fence, should keep the rodents from reaching the garden.

Scarecrows, unless they are windblown, do little to deter problem woodchucks. This rodent seems to recognize danger by things that move. Noise makers may be more effective, but this will probably provide only a temporary fix.

The burrows of groundhogs provide escapes and homes for many animals. Rabbits often seek these hideouts when chased, or when the cold north wind blows. The woodchuck also provides a meal here and there for natural predators such as coyotes and foxes. Unfortunately though, it also has unnatural enemies such as automobiles.

Chapter 8

Wildlife-Related Diseases

Throughout this book you have read about the types of damage and problems that occur when animal and man share habitat. However, animal diseases and some of the parasites they carry are of great importance because they may affect human health or even take human lives. Some wildlife diseases may also have a major impact on certain populations of wildlife species.

We often recognize diseased animals by their reactions. However, sometimes the animal may not carry a disease. Animals are subject to injuries such as bites, broken bones and wounds that could make them appear abnormal. Most of these animals soon become a meal for predators. Nature has a way of ridding the world of sick and injured wildlife. But animal diseases are also a natural occurrence. Parasites that live on animals are likewise nothing unusual.

An article that appeared in a 1995 *Wildlife Society Bulletin* showed human illnesses and fatalities from eleven wildlife-related diseases. Table 19 shows the number of cases that occurred in 1991 and 1992 that affected humans and the number of fatalities that occurred in 1991 (fatalities for 1992 were not available).

Table 19. Number of cases of ten diseases in the U.S. during 1991 and 1992 for which wildlife species may serve as a vector or reservoir. Source: *Wildlife Society Bulletin* 1995, Review of Human Injuries, Illnesses, and Economic Losses Caused by Wildlife in the United States, 23(3):407-414. Data provided by U.S. Centers for Disease Control and Prevention.

Disease	Total Cases 1991	Total Cases 1992	Fatalities 1991
Brucellosis	104	105	0
Encephalitis	1,021	774	142
Leptospirosis	58	54	1
Lyme Disease	9,465	9,895	Unknown
Plague	11	13	0
Psittacosis	94	92	0
Rabies	3	1	3
Rocky Mountain Spotted Fever	628	502	13
Trichinosis	62	41	11
Tularemia	193	159	2

However, humans, pets and livestock can also serve as the vector for some of the diseases in the table. Consequently, wildlife may have contributed to an unknown proportion of these cases.

Before providing information about specific wildlife diseases and parasites, I would like to pass along a few precautions for anyone that handles, or encounters wildlife. First, don't worry about eating a game animal. I have eaten wild game since I was old enough to chew, and have yet to contract anything except a good taste in my mouth. I have suffered from two cases of food poisoning, but each time this came after eating store-bought meat.

I would suggest, however, that you wear rubber gloves when handling wildlife and cleaning game. You should also wear clothing that does not leave any skin exposed. Spraying down with bug dopes will decrease the possibility of some parasites getting to your skin.

It is smart to avoid having contact with animals that do not appear to act normal. A diseased animal may or may not look sick. A wild animal that seems to have little or no fear of humans is one example of abnormal. Each disease affects an animal differently, as you will read in the following pages.

Finally, always dispose of any animal carcass in a timely manner. Should you feel sick or uncomfortable sometime after handling or coming into close contact with an animal, contact your physician.

Please note, however, the possibilities of you contracting an illness from any animal is very remote. On the other hand, it is not out of the question. To learn more about animal diseases and para-sites, please read on. The following information will help you to better understand the risks you face, and those diseases and para-sites which animals contract and/or transmit.

Botulism

Botulism often affects waterfowl, though poultry may also contract the disease. Newcastle Disease, Avian Chorlera and Duck Plague are similar wildlife diseases that may cause death in water-fowl. The external symptoms of these three diseases are quite simi-lar to botulism and lead poisoning.

Widely distributed strains of bacteria that are left to grow in the soil from decomposing animals, birds and fish (this bacteria may also grow in rotting plants when conditions are suitable) can cause botulism. Various types of poisons come from the bacteria, one of which is the most poisonous substance known to man.

Both artificial and natural situations can cause botulism poi-soning. For instance, birds that feed on flies that feed on animal carcasses may die if the insect carries a high level of the toxin. However, piled, rotting waste grain and feed may also host the poisons associated with botulism and attract flies.

When waterfowl are infected with botulism, they lose muscle control. Those in the water may even drown. The disease causes respiratory failure, starvation and dehydration in poultry and waterfowl. The diseased animals also become easy victims for predators. The proper conditions can cause large die-offs in a short period of time. Those who find dead waterfowl should report this to a district biologist or game and fish department. Contact a veterinarian if you experience a large die-off of poultry.

Brucellosis

Also known as Undulant Fever, Brucellosis is caused by several species of bacteria. The infectious disease is often carried by livestock, primarily cattle, goats, horses and pigs. However, many states fear that wild pigs carry and transmit the disease to livestock. This is one reason why many game and fish and health departments consider the wild pig an undesirable species. The disease can also be passed to humans, usually after drinking the raw milk of animals that carry it. Pasteurization has kept the disease under control.

Human symptoms of Brucellosis include chills, fever, and muscle and joint aches. It can also affect the central nervous system. Antibiotics are used to treat the disease in humans. Livestock that contract the disease may have a loss of appetite, decrease of milk supply and sterility. The best way to protect livestock from the disease is to have them inoculated.

Distemper

Most people are somewhat familiar with distemper, simply because our canine friends can contract the disease. However, distemper also affects several carnivores mentioned in this book, such as coyotes, foxes, raccoons and skunks. The disease begins with a virus and is transmitted from one animal to another by direct contact.

Animals with distemper may have a discharge around the eyes. You may also notice an abnormal behavior in the animal. This odd behavior includes aggressiveness or perhaps fearlessness toward humans and appears similar to rabies. The infected animal may also twitch consistently and wander in every direction. Symptoms begin to show up about 8 to 20 days after the animal contracts the disease. About half of the animals that carry distemper will die.

It should be noted that distemper will assist in reducing populations of animals that have become overpopulated. Any animal showing symptoms of the disease should be destroyed to prevent the spread of distemper.

Lyme Disease

Lyme disease affects humans and some animals. It is an infection caused by *Borrelia burgdorferi*, a member of the family of spirochetes, or corkscrew-shaped bacteria (I don't know about you but that sounds Greek to me). The bacteria spreads, however, after a tick bites a host. The carrier is commonly known as the deer tick, or *Ixodes Dammini*. It is common in the north-central and northeastern states. Its close cousin is another deer tick known as *Ixodes pacificus* which resides in many western states. The deer tick feeds on several mammals and birds, but the white-tailed deer seems to be a favorite for Ixodes ticks.

Table 20. Number of cases of Lyme disease reported in the U.S. from 1985 through 1995. Source: Centers for Disease Control and Prevention.

Year	Total Cases
1985	2,748
1987	2,392
1989	8,803
1991	9,470
1993	8,257
1995	11,413

Lyme disease earned its title after it was first recognized in 1975 in Lyme, Connecticut. Today, numerous cases of Lyme disease have been confirmed in the U.S. (Table 20). According to information provided by the Centers for Disease Control, New York reported the most cases through 1995 (31,982). Next in line is Connecticut with 11,200 cases. Other states nearing five figures are New Jersey and Pennsylvania. Alaska and Montana are the only states that have not yet confirmed Lyme disease.

After the deer tick feeds on a deer, it will drop off and lay eggs. These ticks become larvae and usually end up feeding on mice. The larvae may eventually become infected with the disease, and pose the greatest threat to humans during this stage, or the second stage when they become nymphs. The adults, on the other hand, may also carry and transmit Lyme disease to humans, but they are often noticed before the nymphs because they are larger. As for recognizing the deer tick, even the adults are somewhat smaller than the common "dog tick" or "wood tick." Usually, the deer tick will not transmit the disease until it has been attached for about two days.

There are several symptoms of Lyme disease, though diagnosing the disease is seldom easy. In the early stages, you may feel flu-like symptoms, suffering from fatigue, chills, fever, muscle and joint aches and headaches. You may also develop a circular characteristic skin rash. This rash has a bulls-eye effect, in that you will see a round circle close to the bite, and a larger circle surrounding the smaller circle. The rash is often warm but not painful. However, the rash only occurs in some victims. An allergic reaction to a tick bite may cause a similar bulls-eye appearance.

In the late stages of Lyme disease (several weeks, months or even years later), victims often notice mild or painful arthritis in one or more joints. You can also experience nervous system abnormalities such as numbness and pain. Irregularities of heart rhythm may also occur.

Now for the good news. At the time of this writing, a vaccine which will protect you from contracting Lyme disease was currently in the developmental stages. Physicians can also use antibiotics to treat Lyme disease. The earlier a physician detects the disease, the better your chances of a prompt recovery. But even people in the late stages usually have positive responses to antibiotics. Few fatalities occur from Lyme disease. The real problem comes in diagnosing the disease since its symptoms closely resemble

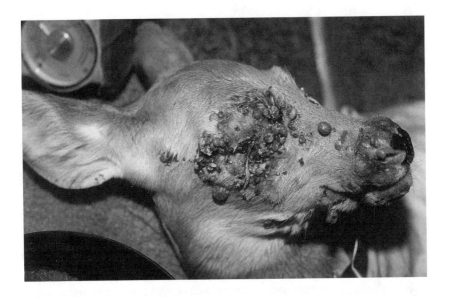

Deer are very susceptible to ticks, particularly the Ixodes type that transmits Lyme disease. This fawn was found blind from the numerous ticks about the head, probably because the doe had neglected it.

other diseases.

Prevention is the key to controlling Lyme disease. Anyone that spends much time in the outdoors from spring to fall is susceptible to ticks, but they can take precautions. You should remove all tall weeds and brush around the yard since ticks love to wait on a host along the edges of dense foliage. You may also want to remove vegetation that attracts deer. Toxic tick chemicals can also be used around the home, garden and lawn to kill ticks (be sure to contact a pest control professional).

Campers, hikers, hunters, fishermen and everyone else who enjoys time in the great outdoors should take necessary precautions before going afield. Whenever possible, wear light-colored clothing so that you can see the ticks. I would also recommend wearing thin, cotton long underwear in addition to your outer clothes. This delays the tick when it attempts to find your skin.

And since ticks often attach onto clothing below the waist, consider tucking your pants into knee-high rubber boots. I would also suggest you apply tape to your pants where they go into your boots to close off any openings. Common sense tells us to wear long-sleeved shirts and hats. You should also avoid walking trails where overhanging foliage brushes against your clothing. Finally, spray skin down with an insect repellent that contains Deet, and clothing with a repellent that contains permethrin.

Today, we have now realized that domestic animals may contract Lyme disease. It has been found in cats and dogs, cattle, horses and other ungulates. Most animals that contract the disease usually show signs of lameness and fever.

Though all this may sound discouraging when you want to enjoy the outdoors, rest assured that your chances of contacting Lyme disease are remote. I am an active outdoorsman for several months of the year, live in a rural area and always take precautions to prevent ticks from attaching to my skin. Yet, family members and I remove several ticks from our skin each year. Thus far, we have managed to escape Lyme disease.

Mange

Both domestic and wild animals can contract mange, though coyotes, foxes, raccoons, squirrels and domestic dogs are particularly susceptible to the disease.

Mange is a contagious skin condition caused by small parasites called mites. Mites have often been compared to chiggers that bury into the skin of humans, causing swelling and itching. When an animal rubs the infected area, though, they develop blisters. The mites then spread to the outer edge of the lesion and begin feeding on healthy skin. If not treated, the mites may affect a large percentage of the animal's body. This can lead to a tremendous amount of hair loss. Squirrels, for instance, usually show the first signs of hair loss around the ears. Weight loss is also common in animals with mange.

Most animals contract mange in the early spring. This is also the time of year when animals carry their thinnest coat of hair or fur. One of the best ways to prevent the spread of mange in wild animals is to destroy them before they spread it to others.

Rabies

Rabies is a viral disease that can attack any warm-blooded mammal, including man. Bats, cats, dogs, foxes, raccoons and skunks often carry this disease. A study in Indiana showed that skunks made up 61 percent of total confirmed rabies cases in a 10-year period. Foxes followed with 6 percent of the cases. The remaining 33 percent included both wild and domestic animals with dogs leading the list. No human cases were reported during the 10-year analysis.

Always pay special attention to nocturnal animals that suddenly become active during daylight hours. Raccoons and skunks in particular seldom venture about during the midday hours, unless they are unhealthy.

Rabies is fatal once symptoms occur. Vaccines will protect people, though, if given immediately after exposure to the disease. Animals that carry rabies often act tame, aggressive and/or depressed, and may bite or scratch others or themselves for no apparent reason. Partial paralysis, sometimes in the lower jaw, and secreting foamy saliva are also common symptoms. However, animals with distemper have similar symptoms. Always contact your game and fish department when a wild animal acts strangely, or veterinarian or local health department if a pet has any of the above mentioned symptoms.

The rabies virus attacks the nervous system. The virus is often transmitted in the saliva and passed on to other animals or humans by biting. However, it can also be transmitted from the animal's mucous membranes (mouth, nose and eyes) if they come into contact with an open wound. Once one animal transmits the disease to another, symptoms may not develop for 10 to 90 days.

An animal suspected of carrying rabies should be killed. The animal should not be shot through the head, though, since officials may need the brain for laboratory testing. The animal carcass should also be destroyed to prevent spreading of the disease to other animals. However, I would suggest you contact the proper authorities (very promptly) before handling any animal that shows symptoms of rabies.

You can protect pets from rabies through regular vaccinations as instructed by your veterinarian and by keeping them from running freely. Protect your children by instructing them not to approach stray or wild animals. You can also discourage wild animals from spending time on your property by frightening them or removing ideal dens and habitat. Finally, I would suggest you not harbor wild animals, even if they appear cute and cuddly. Harboring a wild animal is also against the law in every state and province unless you have obtained a proper permit.

If you or a family member has been bitten or scratched by an animal, clean the wound thoroughly with soap and water. I would also suggest you immediately go to the nearest emergency center or your doctor.

Rocky Mountain Spotted Fever

Ticks are responsible for spreading Rocky Mountain spotted fever to humans. It is the organism called *Rickettsia rickettsii*, transmitted by the wood tick (dog tick) that causes the illness. The disease earned its title after being discovered in the Rocky Mountain region in the late 1800s. Today, the disease has been confirmed in almost every state in the U.S.

Rocky Mountain spotted fever affects humans in the spring and summer months when ticks are active. However, unlike Lyme disease that may take several weeks or months for symptoms to occur, Rocky Mountain spotted fever becomes aggressive quickly. In most cases, symptoms appear within a few days. Early symptoms include headaches and fever. Shortly thereafter, a reddish-colored rash often appears and begins spreading about the body.

The disease is seldom fatal to humans. In fact, only about two percent of those who contract Rocky Mountain spotted fever die from the disease if they receive medical attention. It should be treated when symptoms occur, however. Physicians commonly use antibiotics to treat the disease.

The best way to prevent Rocky Mountain spotted fever is to take precautionary measures against ticks. I would suggest you follow the same guidelines mentioned under Lyme Disease in the preceding pages.

Toxoplasmosis

Toxoplasmosis is a congenital disease caused primarily by the microorganism *Toxoplasma gondi*. The disease is usually identified in humans by lesions of the central nervous system, including the heart, liver, lungs and brain. Toxoplasmosis can lead to blindness and brain damage. Symptoms also include fever and swollen lymph nodes that may resemble the common cold. All warm-blooded animals and birds can contract the disease if they come into contact with the microorganism Toxoplasma gondi. The disease will often run its course without causing any serious effects in humans. However, a pregnant woman who contracts the disease may experience birth defects to the fetus.

Interestingly, about one-fourth of the U.S. population carry toxoplasmosis antibodies in their body. This indicates that these people have suffered from the infection at one time or another. Once you have contracted the disease though, your body usually builds up an immunity to any future occurrence.

Humans can come in contact with the microorganism that causes toxoplasmosis in a number of ways. The parasite is common in many domestic animals such as cattle, hogs, chickens and other livestock. It is believed that most people who become infected do so after eating raw meat or handling meat after slaughter, though some people contract the disease from the feces of domestic cats. Hunters may also come into contact with the parasite that causes the disease after field dressing an animal. Once meat is cooked thoroughly or frozen for a prolonged period, however, the microorganism that causes the disease dies.

Tularemia

Although we have found tularemia in beaver, deer, muskrats and other mammals, the cottontail rabbit has become the most common victim in most regions. For this reason, many refer to the disease as "rabbit fever." The disease has occurred throughout North America, but the Midwest has experienced the highest number of cases.

Tularemia is caused by bacteria, usually spread by biting flies, fleas, mites and ticks. Rabbits that have become infected are usually sluggish when flushed. Rabbit hunters may spot signs of the disease when field dressing the animal. They may see small, pinpoint size white dots on the liver and spleen of infected rabbits. These organs may also appear dark blue and enlarged. Other diseases and parasites can cause similar symptoms, however.

Humans can contract tularemia when they come into contact with ticks, biting flies, rabbits or through eating insufficiently cooked meat. But the possibility of one contracting the disease is quite rare. During a 10-year period in Indiana, only four cases of human rabbit fever occurred. And considering that Hoosier hunters harvest somewhere around 500,000 rabbits each year, one would have to believe that they would never contract the disease.

Human symptoms of tularemia include chills, fever, muscle pains and a sore that does not heal. Antibiotics will treat the disease. It should also be understood that the disease can often run its course without being treated. However, anyone who has signs of rabbit fever should contact a physician immediately.

Occasionally, tularemia will cause large die-offs of rabbits where high populations exist. I would suggest, though, that hunters avoid wasting meat simply because they fear rabbit fever.

Chapter 9

Wildlife Management

Earlier in this book, I discussed various methods for controlling nuisance animals. There were times, though, that I mentioned hunting, trapping and eliminating wildlife habitat as prevention and control methods. It's now time to explain the benefits of hunting and trapping and the need to conserve wildlife habitat whenever possible. Simply stated, this chapter will focus on the necessary tools for managing wildlife.

At one time, the public domain consisted of 1.8 billion acres. In the U.S., this included prime wildlife habitat from the Appalachian Mountains to the Pacific Ocean. Unfortunately, at least for many wildlife species, two-thirds of the public lands eventually went to individuals, industries and the states. On the positive side, though, much of the land that remained was set aside for national forests, wildlife refuges, national parks and other public purposes. The Bureau of Land Management (BLM) currently manages about 272 million acres. BLM also manages wildlife habitat for more than 3,000 species of wildlife.

But BLM cannot accept the responsibility for all wildlife species, even though they have done a spectacular job of preserving

Many animals have depended upon modern game management. Restoration of the wild turkey is one such success story. It benefits from today's regulated harvests and available habitat.

wildlife for our future. When it comes down to the hard facts, it is humans who must preserve habitat.

The majority of our wildlife populations is dependent on the availability of habitat on private lands for their survival. As one fact sheet put it, "Habitat is in short supply." This is true for many animals that we encounter close to our homes. But if a wildlife

Hunting and trapping are considered effective wildlife management tools. Sportsman's license monies and taxes contribute to wise management practices. Photo by Vikki L. Trout.

population is to survive, they must have the same essentials that humans require — food, water and shelter. You cannot increase wildlife populations without providing them with resources. Any increase in habitat, or a given population of animals, is also beneficial for you and I.

Before I provide suggestions for restoring habitat, let me first say a few words about hunting and trapping. Our earliest settlers hunted and trapped animals for food, clothing, shelter and tools. At that time, no laws restricted the number of animals that individuals could harvest. Thus, many species of wildlife were annihilated. Today, the harvest of every animal species is carefully managed to fit the carrying capacity of the lands. I might add, we now see booming populations of many animal species thanks to regulated harvests.

Additionally, sportsmen pour billions of dollars into the economy annually, much of which provides wildlife habitat and wildlife viewing opportunities. The National Rifle Association reported that hunting license monies and taxes have purchased nearly 4 million acres of essential wildlife habitat and have paid for the managing of more than 50 million additional acres.

No doubt, hunting and trapping is a tradition passed down through the generations. Today, about 18 million sportsmen pursue game animals in the U.S. Their regulated harvests protect crops, trees and valuable plant life. Hunting and trapping also provides assistance for controlling nuisance animals. Yet, in some states, voters have had the right to decide if hunting and trapping should be allowed. In most situations, the citizens have voted to allow hunting and trapping.

However, occasionally voters decide against hunting and trapping. Arizona voters banned trapping on public land three years ago. This has led to an increase in coyotes. In fact, shortly before the writing of this chapter, coyotes attacked two children in metropolitan Phoenix. Dr. Bill Morill, a wildlife biologist and Safari Club's conservation director, said conflicts between humans and coyotes in urban areas underscores how coyotes can adapt to living anywhere. "Coyotes have discovered that living in cities means plenty of cover, escape routes and food. But it also can mean that a child or an adult who gets between a coyote and trash, or a dog food bowl, can become the target of a coyote intent on getting its meal," Dr. Morill said.

To say the least, hunting and trapping have nothing to do with declining wildlife populations, though they can reduce the number of nuisance animals when the need arises. It should also be understood that threatened and endangered species are not trapped or hunted. Poachers may occasionally kill threatened or endangered species, just as they kill many animals that are not protected. However, poachers are not hunters. They are criminals. You should never compare hunters and trappers to game law violators.

On the other hand, habitat destruction does play a significant role in the future of each species. We must remember that most animals must adapt to man. I preached heavily on this subject at the beginning of this book. But because many animals rely on a carrying capacity that varies from season to season, we must often respond by supplying habitat. Even a small surplus of habitat near your home will play a major role in the carrying capacity of many animals. Regardless of whether you manage a backyard or several acres of land, you can do plenty to restore habitat.

One method of restoring habitat is to provide artificial homes for animals. An animal may find natural food and water, but if it does not have a home it cannot survive.

For instance, you can supply den boxes for squirrels by taking hollow logs and wiring them to a tree (other critters may also call a den box their home). You can nail a board at the top of the hollow log, and insert a hole near the top of the log for the squirrel to enter. The den box will suit squirrels best if their opening is about 10 feet off the ground. If a hollow log isn't available, simply build a rectangular-shaped box out of plywood and strap it securely to a tree. The box need only have an inside diameter of about 6 to 8 inches. Speaking of plywood boxes, you can also build a 12-inch square box that does not need a top. Simply place it in the ground without covering it with dirt and you will attract rabbits or other ground dwellers.

You can also attract wildlife by planting adequate numbers and varieties of plants. However, these plants must be placed correctly to satisfy wildlife needs. By establishing a perimeter planting of evergreen and deciduous shrubs, you can provide protective lanes for wildlife to use when moving from one place to another. These boundary plantings also provide food and shelter.

Many backyard wildlife specialists suggest planting evergreens next to busy roads because the conifers muffle the sounds of traffic and make good windbreaks. Boundary plantings should consist of those that do not occupy too much space when they mature. Pruning is usually not considered a good idea, since the outer limbs of many shrubs and trees are what produce natural foods for wildlife.

Flowering dogwoods and dwarf fruit trees are excellent choices.

To provide food for wildlife, you might also consider planting a birdseed mixture. It contains buckwheat, millet, sorghum, soybeans and sunflowers. If you plant it thinly in a sunny area, you can produce both food and cover for wildlife. You should also avoid tilling the garden after the harvest. All of your surplus will provide food and cover for wildlife.

The more snow that occurs in a given area, the more cover wildlife needs. Thick honeysuckle is excellent habitat because it provides food and cover. Two or three rows of pine trees also make good windbreaks. In fact, Christmas tree plantations often attract a variety of animals in the winter months.

Herbaceous cover is a necessity for many animals. Herbaceous plantings consist of a variety of foliage that offer seasonal combinations of cover. This can often be created naturally, though, by burning or timber cutting small sections of woods. However, you should avoid burning and cutting trees in areas where only small woodlots exist. You can seed herbaceous cover along grassy waterways, around pond sites and along the borders of crop fields and woodlots.

Three main types of herbaceous cover — grains, grasses and legumes, are most effective for wildlife when sown in strips 30 to 50 feet wide, either individually or better yet in mixtures. When sown near brushy areas, woodland edges or dense fields, grains work very well. Suitable grains include barley, buckwheat, corn, millet, rye and wheat.

Grasses can include sod-forming or clump-forming varieties but are usually seeded with a legume for best results. Good legume species include alfalfa, clover, cowpeas, crownvetch, Korean lespedeza, sericea lespedeza and soybeans

Fields left to grow are also beneficial to wildlife. An Illinois quail study showed that of 707 active quail nests located by researchers, 41 percent were found in idle fields. Pheasants also enjoy undisturbed herbaceous cover for breeding and nesting. A

Michigan study showed that 50 to 81.8 percent of pheasants were in hayfields.

Mowing is a valuable tool for maintaining herbaceous cover. However, you should restrict mowing to certain seasons. Mowing during spring and early summer months is particularly detrimental to ground nesting birds and rabbits. An Illinois study showed extremely high mortality in pheasants because of the mowing of nesting cover. At least 30 percent of the hens were killed at known nest sites. Another 73.4 percent were killed or injured while nesting in hayfields. A study conducted by the U.S. Fish and Wildlife Service indicated that a reduction in mowing resulted in a sharp increase of rabbits at the Patuxent Wildlife Research Center in Maryland.

If you hope to provide suitable habitat for woodland animals, you should not allow livestock to graze through wooded areas. They trample the tree's feeder roots, eat many small woody plants and cause erosion along slopes.

Woodland edges must be allowed to mature. The development of small trees and shrubs will protect valuable timber trees and at the same time provide valuable wildlife habitat. Studies indicate that woodlands with well-developed shrub edges will support up to 95 percent more birds than those without any edge development.

Insects also appreciate woodland edges. They will attract birds such as wild turkey that need these high protein invertebrates for survival. An abundance of protein allows rapid growth for young birds and helps them to develop feathers and wings so they escape from predators.

I would also suggest that landowners of woodlots avoid removing mature oaks and other mast-producing trees. For instance, acorns produced by both white and red oaks provide food for at least 40 mammals and several species of birds. Deer, ducks, grouse, pheasant, quail and wild turkey are but a few of the wildlife species that need acorns. A good mixture of white and red oak is essential.

Nut masts are often affected by weather, but when one oak group fails another may respond.

You should also avoid the clearing of fencelines whenever possible. A clean fenceline may look better, but it does nothing for wildlife. You can also consider piling brush against fencelines. I have practiced this technique for many years just to provide cover for quail and rabbits near my home. The pilings consist of tree limbs, large rocks and stumps. Undesirable trees that do not produce fruits can be cut and added to the brush pile. By piling the debris loosely, or allowing trees to stay put where they fall, you will enable grasses, vines and bramble bushes to grow. The animals will love this diversity of foliage.

In your state or province, there may be cost-share incentives for you to consider if you want to construct and manage wildlife habitat. The types of habitat include everything from windbreaks to wetlands. For more information, contact your game and fish department. You may also get free advice from your county/district cooperative extension agent.

Food, water and shelter are also necessary ingredients for urban animals. In fact, have you ever noticed how many wild animals make cemeteries and parks their home? Several species of birds, as well as rabbits, squirrels, deer and other animals are commonly found in or adjacent to even the smallest sheltered corridors in many metropolitan areas.

Any urban neighborhood can increase wildlife habitat and viewing opportunities by planting shrubs and berry bushes. Drinking water can be added to habitat in a number of ways. However, any animal that becomes dependent upon you for winter food should never be left stranded. Once winter feedings begin, they should continue for the duration of the cold weather until natural foods become available.

Once you have attracted animals to your neighborhood, you may want to avoid inviting them into your home or dwelling. This can be done by following many of the guidelines mentioned in the preceding chapters. Close off chimneys, attic vents or any other openings to keep animals away from where they are not wanted.

I would also like to say a few words about those individuals who become tempted to pick up young animals. Each year many people take it upon themselves to offer their care and home to young creatures. Some simply believe that they are doing the animal a favor. Unfortunately, this is seldom the case. Many young animals that are snatched from a nest or woods are handed a death sentence. Young rabbits are a perfect example. People often find helpless baby rabbits in a nest and find they can't resist these cute and cuddly animals. Statistics show, however, that most rabbits in captivity will die.

On the other hand, there are other animals that can be successfully raised. But even these animals may suffer. Because I have a game breeder's permit and raise white-tailed deer, I receive several calls each spring from individuals who have picked up newborn fawns. I always have to explain that I cannot accept a deer from the wild and ask that they report the fawn to conservation officers. Surprisingly, most of these people claim that they did not see a doe anywhere in the area and assumed the fawn had been abandoned. This is simply not the case. A mother deer, like many other wild mothers, seldom spends every minute with her young. On the contrary, they often separate the youngsters and keep them hidden, going to them only at feeding times. Mature animals also have a fear of man and will avoid contact with humans, even if it means abandoning the youngsters temporarily. Any animal that does leave their young counts on them remaining hidden and unnoticed. The mother will return later to care for them, but only when she does not feel threatened by man.

It is illegal to pick up any wild animal and place it into captivity. The laws governing this act vary in each state and province.

Young animals that are raised by humans will also have to be released some day. For those that have imprinted on man and have no fear of them, the end result can be devastating. For these reasons, any young animal or eggs in a nest should be left alone. There is no better mother than the species of animal that produced the youngsters. John Buhnerkempe, wildlife programs section head for the Illinois Department of Natural Resources, claims that many young animals die within a few days of being picked up because people have no idea of their nutritional requirements. "Those that do survive often are deposited back into the wild without having had the chance to acquire the skills their mothers would have taught them," Buhnerkempe said.

We are fortunate that many animals can adapt to man's habitat. However, we must remember that our habitat only suits some of the animals, some of the time. Not all animals can survive in our habitat, and no animal will flourish if we do not lend a little habitat when necessary.

I will continue doing everything I can to ensure a future for wildlife, while at the same time doing what is necessary to prevent and control wildlife damage. I have enjoyed living in a rural area and viewing several varieties of animals regularly, but I have often found it necessary to practice some of the nuisance animal control methods mentioned in this book. I encourage you to follow similar practices.

Bibliography

Conover, Michael R., Pitt, William C., Kessler, Kimberly K., DuBow, Tami J., Sanborn, Wendy A., *Review of Human Injuries, Illnesses, and Economic Losses Caused by Wildlife in the United States.* Wildlife Society Bulletin 1995, 23(3):407-414

Marion, Wayne R., *Urban Wildlife: Can We Live With Them?* Thirteenth Vertebrate Pest Conference, University of California — Davis in 1988.

Landry, Sarah B., *Peterson First Guides to Urban Wildlife.* Houghton Mifflin Company, 1994.

Smith, Richard P., *Animal Tracks and Signs of North America.* Stackpole Books, 1982.

Animal Damage Control Program Highlights, Miscellaneous Publication No. 1529. U.S. Department of Agriculture, Animal and Plant Health Inspection Service, 1994.

Dahl, T.E. and C.E. Johnson, *Status and Trends of Wetlands in the Conterminous United States, Mid-1970's to Mid 1980's*. U.S. Department of the Interior, Fish and Wildlife Service, Washington, D.C., 1991.

Prevention and Control of Wildlife Damage, University of Nebraska Cooperative Extension, USDA/APHIS/ADC, Great Plains Agricultural Council — Wildlife Committee, 1994.

Minnesota Department of Natural Resources in cooperation with Minnesota Department of Agriculture, *An Overview of Wildlife Damage Programs in the United States*, 1993 report to the Minnesota Legislature.

Nova Scotia Department of Natural Resources, Dan Banks, *When Beaver Become a Nuisance*; Ross Hall, *When Coyotes Become a Nuisance*; Barry Sabean, *When Raccoons Become a Nuisance*; Mark Pulsifer, *When Skunks Become a Nuisance*; Ross Hall, *When White-tailed Deer Become a Nuisance*, Fact Sheets 1992. Gerald Dickie, *When Fish-eating birds Become a Nuisance*; Jenny Costelo, *When Squirrels Become a Nuisance*, Fact Sheets 1995.

Indiana Department of Natural Resources, Division of Fish and *Wildlife, Management Series No. 2, 3, 4, 5, 8, 9, 10, 11, 12, 13*, 1970s publications.

ᗩppendix

U.S. Government Agencies

USDA/APHIS/ADC
P.O. Box 96464
Room 1624, South Bldg.
Washington, DC 20250

USDA/APHIS/ADC
Denver Wildlife Research Center
Bldg. 16, Denver Federal Center
P.O. Box 25266
Denver, CO 80225

USDA/APHIS/ADC
Eastern Regional Office
Suite 370
7000 Executive Center Dr.
Brentwood, TN 37027

USDA/APHIS/ADC
Western Regional Office
Suite 204
12345 W. Alameda Parkway
Lakewood, CO 80228

USDA/APHIS/ADC
Operational Support Staff
4700 River Road, Unit 87
Riverdale, MD 20737

U.S. Department of Agriculture
14th St. and Independence Ave., SW
Washington, DC 20250

USDI Bureau of Land Management
1849 C Street NW, Room 5600
Washington, DC 20240

USDI Fish & Wildlife Service
Interior Building
1849 C. St., NW
Washington, DC 20240

Organizations

International Assn. of Fish and
Wildlife Agencies
444 North Capitol St., NW
Suite 534
Washington, DC 20001

Centers for Disease Control and
Prevention
P.O. Box 2087
Fort Collins, CO 80522

National Trappers Association, Inc.
216 N. Center St.
P.O. Box 3667
Bloomington, IL 61702

National Wilderness Institute
P.O. Box 25766 Georgetown Station
Washington, DC 20007

National Wildlife Federation
1400 Sixteenth St., NW
Washington, DC 20036-2266

National Wild Turkey Federation
P.O. Box 530
Edgefield, SC 29730

Rocky Mountain Elk Foundation
P.O. Box 8249
Missoula, MT 59807

Safari Club International
4800 West Gates Pass Rd.
Tucson, AZ 85745

Wildlife Disease Association
P.O. Box 886
Ames, IA 50010

Wildlife Legislative Fund of America
801 Kingsmill Parkway
Columbus, OH 43229

Wildlife Management Institute
1101 14th Street, NW
Suite 801
Washington, DC 20005

Wildlife Society, The
5410 Grosvenor Lane
Bethesda, MD 20814

Index

European rabbit. *See* Rabbit
Extension Wildlife Specialist 29

Feral cat. *See* Cats
Feral dog. *See* Dogs
Feral pig. *See* Wild pig
Fish-eating birds 63–65. *See also*
    Gulls; Herons
Florida 112
Flying squirrel. *See* Squirrel
Food and Drug Administration 115
Foxes 89–94
    controlling/preventing 92–94
    distribution 89
    feeding habits 90
    killing livestock 87, 91–92
    tracks 85, 91

Gaviota State Park 97
Geese. *See* Waterfowl
Gopher 29, 30
Gray fox. *See* Foxes
Gray squirrel. *See* Squirrel
Great Smoky Mountains National
    Park 73, 101, 130
Ground squirrel. *See* Squirrel
Groundhog. *See* Woodchuck
Grouse 179–180
Gulls 63–65
    controlling/preventing 64–65
    fish consumption 63–64

Habitat management 176–180
Hall, Ross 88
Hawks 58–62
    controlling/preventing 62

killing poultry 62
    northern goshawk 61
    red-tailed 61
Herbaceous cover 178, 179
Herons 63–65
    controlling/preventing 64–65
    fish consumption 63–64
    great blue 63, 64
Hunting 44, 68, 97
    wildlife management 175–176
Hutchings, Eric 87

Idaho 94, 120
Illinois 16, 24, 54, 178, 179, 182
Indiana
    51, 54, 68, 100, 115, 126
Ixodes Dammini. *See* Ticks
Ixodes pacificus. *See* Ticks

Javelina. *See* Wild Pig

Kansas 120
Kentucky
    21, 26, 27, 80, 111, 112

Land Between the Lakes 21
Louisiana 151
Lyme disease 111, 165–168, 170
    prevention 167–168
    symptoms/treatment 166–167

Maine 141
Mange 168–169